The Stony Point Whisker Club

*My travels with Cato
from the Hudson Valley
to midcoast Maine*

By

Don Loprieno

Canard Publishers
Bristol, Maine 04539

For information and purchases, contact
thestonypointwhiskerclub.com

Grateful acknowledgment is made for permission to
quote from the following works:

Morality for Beautiful Girls, Blue Shoes and Happiness,
and *In the Company of Cheerful Ladies* by Alexander
McCall Smith - Random House
"West –Running Brook" by Robert Frost -Henry Holt
Slaughterhouse Five by Kurt Vonnegut –Dell

Cover design and photos by the author

ISBN 978-0-9816644 -0-8

For Cato

Ave Atque Vale, Felis Nobilis

There are more things in heaven and earth, Horatio,
than are dreamt of in your philosophy."

Hamlet, Act I, Scene 5

FOREWORD

The account that follows is a bit difficult to categorize, but I know it isn't fiction. It's about two unlikely companions, who met by chance or design, then journeyed together for nearly fifteen years, sharing all that life had to offer, and sometimes what it withheld. The result is a kind of memoir that addresses, among other things, the issues of identity, accomplishment, failure, regret and resolution. It also seeks to offer some insight into why we humans do what we do, or perhaps fail to do. Lest all this seem too gloomy, there's a great deal about friendship and affection as well; I can also promise a few smiles and a laugh or two along the way.

Someone once jokingly said that a good story had to have a car chase and a happy ending. This story – much of which occurs on a Revolutionary War battlefield, near an 19th century lighthouse and in coastal Maine - doesn't have a car chase, but it does have what might be described as a happy ending. The book concerns a few main characters – one or two really - and at least one important animal, but, at the risk of making two very flattering (and invidious) comparisons, that's a bit like saying that *The Old Man and the Sea* is about a fish and *For Whom the Bell Tolls* is about a bell.

The playwright Oscar Wilde was once asked by reporters if his new play would be a success. He replied, "Gentlemen, it is already a success. It's merely a question of whether the audience will be a success." Setting aside Wilde's hubris and reputation for witty remarks, there's some truth in his observation. What this book is about will be affected by what readers themselves bring to the story, based on their own experiences. It is hoped that they will interpret the story in such a way as to see it as more than just a personal account, and that the individuals involved and the events described go beyond a particular time and space and have a broader application to other people in similar situations.

Writing any book is not easy; this one has been more difficult than most, being almost a journey in itself, but I have not traveled alone. It was made less difficult with the help of my wife, Page Lockhart, who also shared much of what happened. In addition, Ellie King graciously agreed to read the manuscript through several incarnations, my niece, Lily Lockhart, once again displayed her skill at unraveling the intricacies of photo software and solving technical problems long distance, and my daughter Nora proofread the final version.

I've also been very aware of the presence of my faithful friend Cato, who's been looking over my shoulder, so to speak, guiding in his quiet, helpful way, offering a few words of unspoken advice, and – unless I'm greatly mistaken – nodding his approval on a fairly regular basis. With his keen editorial acumen, he's also suggested that I include some humor or, as he might put it, "make it funny." I have done my best to do just that.

A feline also plays a prominent role in this account. Those who might now be thinking that this book is "only" about a cat should be aware of the "only" word in our language, which belittles whatever term follows it. One could also say that the book is "only" about people or "only" about events. "Only" isn't just a choice of words or a matter of semantics. Like all language, it shapes our thoughts, providing a structure for the values we hold and the actions we take.

Those who have had long-term relationships with animals know first hand that a bond of trust and understanding often occurs, one that can be of a different quality than that found between members of our own species. Others will think differently, feeling that a human life takes precedence over any other, and that interactions between people are more important. That is, of course, a particularly human point of view, and it's a perfectly natural distinction to make.

I understand. I used to feel that way myself. I don't anymore.

Don Loprieno
Bristol, Maine
Spring, 2008

1

Job of a Lifetime

Anyone who's ever been trapped in a dead end job for so long that it seemed like a prison sentence will understand exactly how I felt. I'd re-invented myself more times and in more ways than I could remember, but still no reprieve was on its way, no improvement or even change seemed possible.

Then, in April 1992, I was appointed to manage Stony Point Battlefield, a state historic site in New York. It was located on the west bank of the Hudson River and consisted of a rocky, ninety-acre promontory surrounded on three sides by water, and complimented by panoramic views of Haverstraw Bay. Its historic significance lay in the fact that the site was comprised of an 18th century battlefield and a 19th century lighthouse. My wife Page and I would live on the grounds in a rustic clapboard – and – fieldstone Adirondack style house, complete with a covered front porch, an expansive living room with fireplace, several upstairs bedrooms, but, alas, only one bathroom! It was more space than we were used to, certainly more than we needed, perhaps more than any two people should have.

It was also the only habitable structure on the grounds. Set back from the bustle of modern life by an entrance gate and a tree-lined winding road about a quarter mile long, our new home could easily be mistaken for the manor house of a private estate. The peninsula of Stony Point was situated approximately twenty five miles north of Manhattan and twelve miles south of West Point, and was, in fact, almost a land island; the secluded setting of the house amid its surrounding environment created the appearance of an autonomous political and geographical entity – governed, of course, by laws and regulations promulgated beyond the gate.

Living and working in the same place would be a new experience for me. Like most people, my previous employment had the usual separation between job and home. The situation at Stony Point was different: no more long commutes, just a simple five-minute walk up the hill to the museum and I could start my day. Of course, I'd heard the expression "living above the store," but never having done that before, I had no real comprehension of the distance we all need between what we do and who we are, and the lack of privacy that occurs when that separation isn't maintained. That realization would come much later.

Overall, the situation I found myself in was one that many readers can relate to, because though they may never have managed a historic site, they've probably had a similar experience. I was in charge of a workplace where I tried to meet performance standards set by myself and others, make intelligent, thoughtful decisions that would have a positive effect on all concerned, and attempt not only to achieve specific goals, but also to accomplish them in a way that showed competence, ability and sound judgment. Stony Point was all that and more; it was also a long-delayed promotion, something everyone can appreciate, particularly if it's offered in recognition of one's achievements or potential. In my case, I was beginning to think it would never happen. When it finally did, I was ecstatic.

The battlefield's relative isolation made it subject as well to enhanced local control in the form of a newly - arrived site manager. I wanted to improve the historical property so that it became all that it could be, while, at the same time, demonstrating the many benefits of a limited benevolent dictatorship – at least that was my plan.

Because the grounds were rich in military and maritime history, interpreting that history – teaching it, if you will – to the public was another important aspect, one that greatly appealed to me because of my background and experiences. In high school, I'd had been exposed to the influence of several inspiring teachers, whose knowledge and ability to impart it had always impressed me and ultimately led me to attend and complete college, the first in my family to do so. After graduation, I taught for nearly ten years in the mid Hudson Valley, and one of the first things I learned was that a good teacher always had a keen interest in his subject, one that was genuine and couldn't be faked. All the techniques in the world would be useless without that authentic appeal and enthusiasm, which could then be conveyed to others.

That was especially true of history – a topic I've always enjoyed, though its attraction is often diminished by a mistaken focus on dates, places, and obscure clauses in even more obscure treaties. Two thirds of history, after all, is the word "story" and unless the story is told in human terms about people very much like ourselves who behaved very much as we might in the same circumstances, then the relevance of the past could easily be lost. To me, history wasn't dull or far removed from the present, but vital, real and important. If history wasn't that, then neither was memory or experience.

For me, then, Stony Point was the job of a lifetime. In a sense, I'd be in a classroom again, but one without walls. Moreover, when I arrived, the battlefield was facing an identity crisis – it was rapidly changing from a historic site to a park, and beginning to be viewed as just "a pretty place." To alter that perception, I was determined to tell the story of the battle in ways that could transcend the past and make the participants on both sides as real as possible. The British and American soldiers who had fought on these grounds during the Revolutionary War were, after all, human beings just like ourselves, governed by the same motives, attributes and shortcomings.

I also wanted to relate the story of the Stony Point lighthouse keepers who kept lonely vigil from 1826 to 1925, when the lighthouse was decommissioned. From my point of view, the military and maritime aspects of Stony Point were two halves of the same exciting history. Though light keepers and soldiers may seem at first to have little in common, a closer look revealed a number of similarities. Both shared the attributes of loyalty, fortitude, perseverance, dedication to duty, and, if need be, putting one's own life at risk for others.

I wanted to make all this history come alive, not forgotten and relegated into a dustbin of time and space as irrelevant and unimportant. I'd also felt for some time that truth was not only stranger than fiction; it was more interesting. Almost anyone with a little imagination and some dramatic ability can invent a good story, but when a story about some event that occurred in the past also happens to be true because it's supported by facts and witnesses, then it's history. In that sense, Stony Point was very fertile ground indeed.

2

Pride Goeth Before a Fall

The battlefield became the setting for the events that followed, including the introduction of what could be called this narrative's main character, not to mention the founding of the Stony Point Whisker Club. My presence was an essential element as well: if I hadn't been there, everything would have happened differently, or more likely, not have happened at all. Therefore, in addition to the reasons already stated, it should be explained that the overriding consideration behind my decision to become site manager and which captured my imagination was the chance to be involved not in history from books, but where it actually happened.

The battle of Stony Point, for instance, was a set piece of military strategy, and had been fought in 1779 – two years after Saratoga and two years before Yorktown. In a little less than half an hour, British fortifications, along with fifteen pieces of artillery and a garrison of over five hundred men, fell into American hands, despite the fact that another British fort was less than a mile away across the Hudson, and fighting ships of the Royal Navy patrolled the river in between. The battle plan which achieved this victory had been devised by Washington himself, and improved upon by Brigadier General Anthony Wayne, who also led the troops during the assault.

The tactics admirably suited the situation. In late May 1779, after taking an American fort at Verplanck's Point on the Hudson's opposite bank, the British captured Stony Point and began constructing two sets of defenses including artillery positions, additional barriers made of fallen trees, and three-sided fortifications intended for infantry support.

A fatal flaw in these defenses – one which the Americans would soon exploit - was that they were open in the rear and therefore vulnerable to encirclement. Nonetheless, the Royal Navy maintained control over the river, and the British still had two forts that could provide mutual support. The King's troops at Stony Point also commanded the high ground, not only overlooking the Hudson on the east but also the landward side to the west, from which an enemy attack was most likely to be launched.

At a time when major rivers were equal to modern highways and control of them in wartime was critical, Stony Point had vital military significance. Along with Verplanck's Point, it marked the entrance to the Hudson Highlands, where the river narrowed significantly, requiring enemy ships to sail well within the limited range of 18th century artillery. Stony Point was also a terminus for the King's Ferry, a strategic river crossing, and was located only twelve miles south of the American fortress at West Point, where the river was blocked by a log boom and links of iron- a formidable obstacle occasionally referred to as "General Washington's watch chain."

For all these reasons, the British could not be allowed to remain a threatening presence at Stony Point. After an extended period of reconnaissance, Washington's plan was devised. A daytime attack would severely reduce the crucial element of surprise and expose the Americans to heavy fire. An attack at night, however, could be undetected until it was too late, and, at same time, render the artillery ineffective because these smoothbore, line-of-sight weapons were useless in the dark. To safeguard the American approach from enemy resistance, a diversionary force would simulate a conventional attack by firing volleys in the center of the peninsula and draw British attention. This ruse would divert the enemy's defenses from the real assault launched by two columns, each armed only with unloaded muskets and fixed bayonets. One column would sweep around the north side of the peninsula while the other would wade through the shallow waters of Haverstraw Bay to the south and ascend the high ground where the main fortifications lay. To avoid confusion, the Americans would wear pieces of white paper in their hats and shout the watchword " The Fort's Our Own" when they entered the British positions.

At approximately 12:20 A.M. during the dark and windy early morning hours of July 16, 1779, this brilliant plan was put into effect. Though the British response was a valiant one, it was also uncoordinated and misdirected. The swiftness of the American advance, combined with the diversion in front and the blustery weather – which not only prevented enemy ships in the river from playing an active role but also restricted the passage of British reinforcements from across the Hudson - overwhelmed the beleaguered garrison whose open defenses offered virtually no protection. Thirty-five soldiers were killed on both sides, with the dead buried somewhere on the grounds, where they remain to this day.

The first part of the American goal – to capture Stony Point – had been achieved, but Washington knew that possession of both forts was necessary to regain military control. His plan to attack Verplanck's Point, however, went awry, leaving him no choice but to abandon Stony Point before the British regrouped and retook it by force. Nonetheless, the victory thwarted enemy intentions while greatly improving American morale at a time when the Revolutionary War had already dragged on for four years with no end in sight. Five months later, in December 1779, the British shifted their efforts to Charleston, South Carolina, a decision that would ultimately lead to the surrender of Lord Cornwallis at Yorktown in 1781. The significance of the capture and brief occupation of Stony Point is perhaps best understood by the fact that of only eleven medals individually designed and awarded by Congress for valor during the eight year struggle for independence, three were given to officers at Stony Point – all for a battle that lasted less than thirty minutes.

The Stony Point lighthouse was the maritime half of the site's rich history. Built in 1826, a year after the opening of the Erie Canal linking the Hudson with the Great Lakes, the lighthouse was necessary because of increased commercial traffic, and, like all lighthouses, was constructed near a navigational hazard. In this case, its purpose was to mark the entrance to the Hudson Highlands where the river's course becomes narrow and tortuous, in contrast to the river's widest expanse at Haverstraw Bay in the south. This dramatic and sudden change – a rapidly constricting shoreline combined with the rocky landmass of the Stony Point peninsula jutting into the confined passage - could be dangerous to the inexperienced helmsman, particularly at night.

For nearly one hundred years, the lighthouse was operated by eight keepers, including three members of the Rose family – Alexander, his wife Nancy, and their daughter Melinda. When her husband died in 1857, Nancy herself kept the light for another 47 years – trimming the lantern wicks, polishing the lens, ringing the bell in foggy weather, cleaning and maintaining the lighthouse. Each day, regardless of weather or conditions, the lamps were lighted at dusk and extinguished at dawn, throwing a beacon of light across the waters, a reminder that someone was always there to send a warning, an admonition to be watchful and safe. It is a testament to steadfast and faithful dedication to duty that the only wreck which occurred at Stony Point during the nearly one hundred years of its operation was that of the steamer *Poughkeepsie*, which ran aground in 1901 with no loss of life.

I was fully cognizant of this two-fold history and the peninsula's unique character, and I hoped to encourage visitors to appreciate their significance, particularly that of the battle, which was the primary reason for the site's preservation.

Short in duration, momentous in outcome, the battle of Stony Point needed to be remembered and honored. I had a sense as well – one that would be more fully developed in later years – that the energy of that battle, the courage, fear, adrenaline, and the sheer, concentrated violence – had somehow not dissipated

17

despite the passage of time, but was still present in some form that I could neither recognize nor fully understand. I also felt – and still do - that if all battlefields were so remembered and honored, then perhaps the alternative of war, its harsh realities often obscured by parades and political bombast, would not be so readily chosen as a resolution for conflict.

Most of us are compelled to live by other people's rules. The land island of Stony Point, however, was not only an opportunity to relate its history, but also to create, within reason, my own rules, and to establish a small version of an ideal society. In retrospect, I like to think that most decisions made at this time were positive ones, but I'd be less than candid if I claimed some sort of perfection or infallibility. We all want to look good, we all want to feel important, we all seek some measure of approval – I was no exception to these desires, and they were often a strong motivation in my actions. In my zeal, however, I began to think in proprietary terms about a house and property that I could never own, but which I somehow thought of more and more as mine.

I'd also overlooked the ancient maxim that power corrupts – and, if I'd forgotten that, there was always good old hubris – not to mention "Pride Goeth Before a Fall." That was inexcusable for one so interested in history – and it would soon lead to an unfortunate consequence.

3

Without a Second Thought

Someone once referred to Theodore Roosevelt's need to be the center of attention by describing him as "the bride at every wedding, the corpse at every funeral." So it was with me. If there was a tour at Stony Point, I had to lead it. If there was a special event, I had to introduce it. If there was a school group, I had to be the person in charge. There was no point, after all, in managing my little world in the best possible way if no one knew who had done it. I had my reasons.

As a kid, I was exposed to a family life that was unpredictably volatile, leaving me with the strong impression that things could easily get out of hand at any moment; as I got older, that experience led me to believe that taking control of events and situations was very important. And because the adults around me sometimes made some very poor decisions, I became distrustful of authority in general, inside the home and without. Years later, when I had some of the authority that adults around me had misused, it did not escape my sense of irony that I, too, would make some very poor choices.

Doing each task or project carefully and well was especially important to me because I'd also been brought up to believe that whatever I did wasn't good enough; it's a lesson you don't dispute if you learn it from your parents at an early age. Eventually I realized that while it seemed I could never meet their expectations (though, of course, I continued to try) I could at least show everyone else how adept and organized I was. Like the butler in one of Bob Dylan's songs, I had something to prove.

In any case, as far as I could see, some competence in everyday affairs was certainly needed. The world in general and the nation and state of which I was a part were seldom run to my satisfaction. Laws were passed that were inequitable and shortsighted, political decisions were made that often seemed unfair and unjust, taxes were spent in ways that were foolish and imprudent. The world beyond the gate at Stony Point sometimes made me feel like the old soldier who, after many years of service, decided not to reenlist, but then returned a few days later. Why have you come back, he was asked. Because there's no one in charge out there, he answered.

Stony Point was my chance to run my small part of the universe as I thought it should be. The extent of my domain even included the natural world – or so I thought. For example, there was a pond near the front gate. It was a fine pond, but it needed something. It needed ducks. I would supply them. I had no choice. Wild ducks, alas, may have noticed the pond, but they never lighted there. After all, why should they when there were many larger ponds and lakes near by – not to mention the width and breadth of Haverstraw Bay? For worldly ducks or the young who've just tasted of freedom, it was a little like the appeal of a brightly lighted big city as compared to the drab isolation of a very small town.

I bought some baby ducks at a local farm supply store, transported them to the battlefield, and for a while, kept them in the basement of my house. It was a relief to all – especially the ducks - when they had grown enough to be moved outdoors where fencing had been erected so they wouldn't wander off and a shed had been built to confine them at night so they'd be safe. They were now my ducks and soon as they could fly, they would settle on the site pond, which only lacked their presence to be complete. That was the plan, though, in retrospect, I don't recall communicating that to the ducks. I had hoped that nature would take its course, and the ducks would take to the pond like – well, like ducks to water.

However, as they grew, they made an important discovery: they had wings - wings which, if properly employed, could carry them over and above their confinement to the world beyond and a freedom hitherto unknown. This insight was acquired by one lone duck of obviously advanced intelligence – or at least advanced development - who flapped over the pen into the trees nearby, and signaled the others to escape. His fellow detainees soon received the message and, one by one, departed over the fencing, into the sky, circling overhead, but not going where they were intended. The mighty Hudson – called "The River That Flows Two Ways" because its fresh water currents flowing south from the Adirondacks commingles with salt water flowing north from the Atlantic Ocean - held far greater appeal than what, from a few hundred feet up, must have seemed like a very uninteresting puddle. The ducks didn't want to be just ducks in a small pond. I couldn't blame them.

Because they were my ducks on my battlefield, it goes without saying they were subject to constant vigilance. If I couldn't see them from where I was, I'd ask someone who could. I queried my wife, the groundskeepers, the staff, almost anyone who could vouch for their wellbeing. It got to be predictable and probably very annoying. It was difficult to convey to those who didn't understand that if these ducks became injured or sick, the onus would fall on me; I was personally responsible for the creatures I had imported into my preserve. Like Tony in the Soprano series that would air many years later, I was concerned with their welfare. They were under my protection, a term that Tony would have appreciated and might well have used himself.

That included, of course, guarding them against predators, though that did not seem to be a problem. A family of foxes had been spotted at the other end of the battlefield below the lighthouse near the water, but they were absorbed in raising and playing with their young. An occasional coyote would lope through the grounds from time to time, but apparently posed no threat. Other animals on the scene ranged from the usual squirrels and chipmunks to several kinds of birds, including geese and a number of majestic bald eagles that occasionally hunted near the river. It was, it seemed to me, a small menagerie comprising an idyllic Eden in the style of Edward Hicks's painting *The Peaceable Kingdom*, with animals and humans living beside each other without strife or conflict. It was a quiet, tranquil setting where the lion would indeed lie down with lamb.

One day in early May 1993 when the site was closed to the public, I had to leave for a meeting. Being away always caused me some distress. I loved the quiet of the site when there was no activity, and I'd arranged for staff to be off when there was no public, in order to maintain the peaceful atmosphere. I hated to head off into the noisy and chaotic world past the gate, and I felt anxious, as I always did, that I couldn't remain behind to enjoy the pristine setting and also be on the premises in case I was needed. It was tough being indispensable.

That feeling of anxiety, combined with what I now know to be a false sense of obligation and a real need for control, soon led to an act that I didn't think much of at the time but have regretted ever since. Spying a strange cat perched on a hill above my ducks and watching them very closely, I defended my feathered friends by killing the cat with a rifle shot. It was not first animal I had killed - but it would be the last.

At the time, I'd considered myself a rational, intelligent person, fairly well educated and compassionate to those less fortunate (at least in theory if not practice) - basically a good person, not perfect, but still one who could think through a situation and come to an informed decision, yet I was able to kill without a second thought. Second thoughts would come later. They would be in the form of a small creature who would be brought to our door one day and stay for nearly fifteen years.

4

Something in a Small Basket

It was Memorial Day Weekend 1993, and Stony Point Battlefield was a very busy place. A special event was being held, and visitors were everywhere – in the parking lot, up the hill at the museum where the event was already in progress, or by the lighthouse, enjoying the view of the Hudson River. Some were also at the site house, even though it was identified as a private residence, but that wasn't unusual.

As they drove to the parking lot, visitors had to pass right by the house, and some always mistook it for the museum. Historically, they had a point; in 1905, the house *was* the museum as well as being the living space for the "keeper," the term by which the site manager was originally known. The keeper and his family lived upstairs and had a kitchen in the basement, while the main floor called "The Relic Room" was open to the public. Among other items, it contained a small bronze mortar captured during the battle and a portrait of Brigadier General Anthony Wayne, who had led the American forces.

By 1936, however, the Works Progress Administration, popularly known as the W.P.A., helped construct a new museum on higher ground some distance away, but some visitors never got that far They would occasionally park their cars in the lot below the house, cut across the lawn to our residence, and, thinking that it must be the museum, casually walk in, sometimes without knocking. Once my wife Page, clad only in a robe, had just emerged from the shower on the main floor and encountered one of these visitors in our living room. Needless to say, Page was somewhat startled, and the visitor was more than somewhat embarrassed.

On this busy late May weekend, the same situation seemed to be occurring again. A woman was standing at the door of the house, and had rung the bell. I was outside, and approached from behind, ready to tell her – in a professional, diplomatic manner and hopefully without the mild annoyance I often felt on such occasions – that the museum was up the hill, that this building was a private residence, and that it was closed to the public, as a nearby sign clearly stated. One of the things I had learned about visitors was that regardless of what a sign said - no matter how large it was, no matter how clear its language, no matter how prominent its location - most people would claim they hadn't seen it.

So I thought I knew what was happening, but, as it turned out, I was mistaken. Page, having heard the bell ring, was already on her way as I was about to politely point out to the woman at my door that this was not the museum. As she turned to face me, I saw that she'd been carrying something in a small basket, which she now began to offer to me and Page, who had arrived on the scene. Cupped in the woman's hands was a tiny and lively ball of animated fur - a very small kitten, obviously anxious and afraid, meowing in its distress, its fate now in the hands of strangers, for good or ill. It had been found on the battlefield, one of a litter, and was being offered for adoption, the others already having been given away. Page had just begun to refuse because she knew of my allergies to many things, including cats. Besides we were not planning to have a pet, especially a feline.

So if logic and experience had prevailed, we would have rejected the creature now being presented to us. The poet Alexander Pope once compared human decisions to a ship, with the sails as emotion propelling the vessel and the rudder as reason, directing its course. One look at the long-haired orange tabby kitten with his sky blue eyes caused me to drop the rudder, puff up the sails and let my feelings run before the wind – damn the allergies, full speed ahead! We'll take him, I said.

Because we had agreed to accept the kitten, we went overnight from a couple to a family. Our first thought was that the tiny creature was probably hungry, but when he was offered solid food, it became clear that he was not yet weaned. I went out to get a bottle and other cat supplies while Page cut a clean sponge into a soft spike and used it to give him some milk. He was ravenous. I returned with a baby's bottle, complete with nipple. It wasn't intended for felines, but the kitten instinctively began to drink from it.

I was already showing some allergic reaction, so the kitten was put in the spare bedroom with a litter pan and water at bedtime. During the night Page checked on him, gave him some special kitten milk from the bottle, and cuddled him until he fell asleep. This pattern continued for a few weeks, during which time he learned to eat kitten chow soaked in kitten milk, and somewhat later, canned cat food. He soon became very active, enjoying the interior of the house, but vastly preferring the outdoors, and like all kittens, trying to get into the smallest spaces. We panicked when he crawled under the deck, which was only inches off the ground; after I managed to retrieve him, I kept the access points blocked.

Over time, my allergies lessened, although they never completely went away. However, priorities had been established – the cat's needs came first. After all, he was only a very small kitten, he could not be returned – in any case, we didn't know who to return him to – and we had already made a commitment that we intended to keep, no matter how often sneezes or runny noses tried to interfere.

From the beginning, the kitten enjoyed playing with the simplest of objects - an old rawhide shoelace, a piece of string, a ball of yarn - and he began to explore what amounted to his own private estate. The forsythia bush near our house became one of his favorite haunts, and as he grew older he wanted to stay out all night. Each evening at bedtime we spent an hour or so wheedling him back into the house for the night because we didn't think he was safe outside. He thought otherwise, and eventually we gave up and let nature take its course. We occasionally worried about him, but he always came home (when he was good and ready) through his personal cat door that we'd provided.

He also liked to explore and play in the house. He liked small, dark spaces too, and soon went on what we called "closet patrol" or "basement patrol" sniffing and scenting every nook and corner. If we couldn't find him anywhere, we learned to open doors and look inside. There he'd often be, looking back at us with a bemused

27

expression but never making a sound. Was it a game he was playing? If so, he must have been amazed at how long it took us humans to figure out where he was. He also dazzled us with his antics, racing madly about the house, leaping into the air after a feathered toy, chasing objects pell mell across the floor.

He was true to his nature, just as we humans are to ours. As befits a feline, he was fastidious in his grooming, and worked hard to develop and perfect his hunting skills, pouncing with incredible grace and agility a far greater distance than we could have imagined. He was a wonder to behold and made us laugh out loud – chipmunks and other prey, of course, had a different response, although chipmunks soon learned how to play dead, and scamper off to safety as soon as the cat became distracted.

Once, when I was at the house for lunch, I heard a ruckus upstairs; he had pursued a mouse into our bedroom, and the chase was fast and furious. When I'd finished eating, I went back upstairs because suddenly, all was quiet. I didn't know what to expect, but the change in noise level had been sudden and dramatic. I discovered why when I reached the bedroom. The cat was napping peacefully under the bed, with his quarry nowhere in sight. I looked under the cedar chest a few feet away; in a space about an inch high there was the mouse – also fast asleep. The frenzied chase had ended in a standoff, with both prey and predator taking a much-needed break. Until then, for me the phrase "playing cat and mouse" had been just an expression.

At first we didn't know what name to give our kitten. We experimented with "Fuzzball" (an apt description but a little too cute) and "Junior" (though he didn't look at all like me). Finally, thinking that a cat who lived on an 1779 battlefield should be called something appropriate for the period, we decided on Cato, after an 18th century play by Joseph Addison about a famous statesman of ancient Rome. In the usual manner of most pet owners, we had other names for him as well. He was also known as Mr. Puss and Cato P. Cat – the "p" of course standing for "perfect." In jest, we'd often call Cato "a beastly beast" and picture him doing "beastly things" (whatever that meant) and, of course, thinking "beastly thoughts" unlike us superior humans. He and I were also charter members of The Whisker Club, an organization for which our respective hirsute endowments provided eminent qualification. It was, as you might imagine, a very exclusive society; by mutual agreement, its membership was permanently limited to exactly two.

Cato soon responded when he heard his name, and would saunter toward us, bushy tail erect. There is nothing to quite equal the feeling we got when we saw Cato a hundred yards away, called him, and watched as he ran to us. Each time it happened, it was a combination of winning a contest and falling in love.

Of course, there were just as many times when we called and called, only to spot him sitting on a tree limb or under a bush in daytime or sometimes at night in the grass just at the edge of the flashlight's reach, watching us complacently but declining to come in just yet.

Though there were very few other animals on the battlefield, Cato did have one encounter with a skunk and got sprayed. We tried all the folk remedies, but his thick undercoat held the smell until we bought a commercial product and soaked him in it. The odor finally left, but in the meanwhile Page found herself gagging every morning as Cato persisted in climbing on the bed and snuggling up to her face.

On the Fourth of July, 1994, when he was just over a year old, Cato crawled up onto Page's chest, fluid running from his nose and mouth. He was clearly but mysteriously very sick. Despite the holiday, we found an animal hospital that was open for emergencies, and, with many misgivings, had to leave him there overnight. He was prescribed a course of antibiotics for weeks and recovered, but the veterinarian was never able to diagnosis the underlying problem. The medication was a liquid that apparently tasted good, because he would sit obediently at my feet to take it from a spoon. The bond that was beginning to be forged between human and cat was made stronger.

Cato would often accompany us on site walks after hours when the gate was closed. He especially enjoyed going with me up to an area near the lighthouse and surveying our domain. At the end of a working day, during that delicious time in summer between late afternoon and early evening, Cato and I would often head for the observation platform near the peninsula's highest point. There, he and I would savor each other's quiet company as we enjoyed the view of the gleaming white tower of the Stony Point lighthouse framed against the opposite shore, and the glistening waters of Haverstraw Bay, the Hudson's widest point, looming to the south. It was a peaceful, idyllic setting that appealed to both of us. Page worked in Kingston, about an hour's drive north, and when she came home to the battlefield and found no one at the house, she knew where we'd be and often walked up the hill to join us. Her presence meant, of course, that any meeting of the Whisker Club that had been in progress would have to be immediately suspended, but she was welcome nonetheless.

On Mondays and Tuesdays when the site was closed to visitors, Cato would often go up the hill to the museum with me and frolic inside the office as I caught up on paperwork. One of his favorite games was rolling pencils off my desk after I'd placed them there. I'd pick them up; he'd focus all of his concentration lest they make a sudden move, and then attack, knocking them, one by one, to the floor. Then we'd start all over again until all the pencils had been subdued.

On other days, he would occasionally greet visitors, and once tried to catch a wild turkey, whose abrupt and lumbering takeoff into the nearest tree resembled the ungainly flight of a huge cargo plane and startled all of us, particularly Cato. Once, during a torrential downpour, Cato was nowhere to be found. He'd gone out sometime before and was sure to get drenched unless we could lure him home. We called for him over and over while the heavens opened, complete with high winds whipping across the battlefield. We finally realized that, even if he could hear us, Cato was too savvy to respond until the weather cleared. Sure enough, when the storm abated, here was Cato, trotting down the hill, wondering what all the fuss was about. He'd found his own shelter and was only slightly damp. Nonetheless, his purring told us he enjoyed being dried off by the towel we threw over him, thus establishing a custom from which we never deviated. From that day on, Cato expected us to appear, towel in hand, whenever he came in from the rain, even if he was only damp. It became a special treat that we enjoyed as much as he did.

In rainy or snowy weather, he loved to sit on the big stone half-walls that bordered our deep front porch. At night, he'd come and go through his own door, and often when we'd be returning after dinner out, his furry rump and the glint of his eyes would be caught in our headlights as he raced toward home to get there before we did, anticipating the fish or chicken leftovers we'd bring him from our restaurant meal. Page's mom once jokingly described Cato as "the spoiled, only child of elderly parents." Well, of course, I resented the word "elderly" - whaddaya mean "elderly?" I would mutter to myself – and while it was true that Mr. Puss was very much like the child that Page and I chose not to have, I'd never felt that apologies or even explanations were necessary for the attention and love he received. Some people would understand it, some wouldn't. I had been one of those who hadn't, but now I knew better. Looking back now, I realize that it was the first and only time that I had been given the choice of accepting – or refusing – the responsibility for a life; to nourish and care for it, to make certain that it was protected and safe from harm, and ultimately to give thanks for its presence.

Cato was the spirit of affection, the soul of playfulness, the epitome of friendship, the essence of quiet comradeship – all embodied in the form of a cat. Soon, we couldn't imagine life without him. We wondered how our good fortune had come about, why he had not been brought to one of the many other houses outside the battlefield grounds, why he had come to our door instead.

One day, I realized how it had happened, and I began to understand and regret the hurt I had caused. With my experience and background, I could not help but know that the past would always remain fixed and unalterable, that it could never be changed. It wasn't exactly news either. In the 11th century, the Persian poet Omar Khayyam put it best:

> *"The Moving Finger writes; and, having writ, Moves on:*
> *Nor all your Piety nor Wit*
> *Shall lure it back to cancel half a line*
> *Nor all your Tears wash out a Word of it."*

What had been done could never be undone – that was clear – and though I'd read this passage before, the past had never weighed as heavily on me as it did now.

Haverstraw Bay from Stony Point Battlefield

View south from Stony Point Battlefield

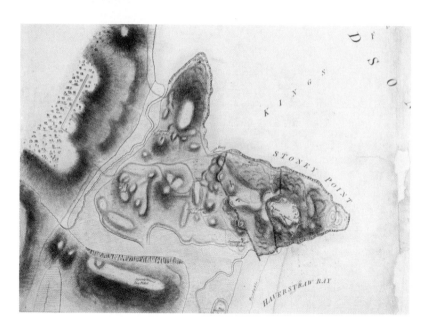

18th century map of Stony Point peninsula

Site manager's residence, Stony Point Battlefield

*Cato in May 1993. He was so young he had
to be weaned with a baby's bottle.*

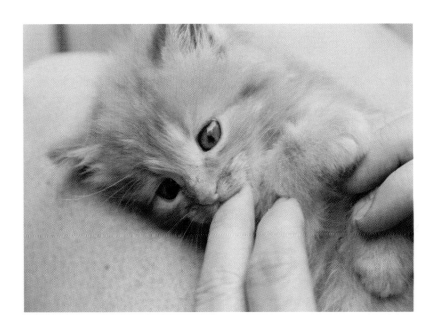

My Ducks

Cato on snow patrol – Stony Point Battlefield

Page and Cato in our side yard at Stony Point

Cato and friend

The Stony Point lighthouse, oldest on the Hudson River, built in 1826, restored and relighted in 1995.

Battlefield staff, August 2000. The author is on the right.

Cato on his private estate
Stony Point Battlefield

After William Ten Eyck, Stony Point Battlefield's first keeper, died in 1916, his wife Sarah (1857-1944) was appointed in his stead and served another 28 years. Cato may well have been a descendant of the unidentified feline pictured here with her.

5

The Origins of Indifference

The cat I had killed to protect my ducks had been Cato's mother. Her death at my hands had shattered an animal family and caused her kittens to be abandoned until they'd been discovered by the unknown woman who rescued them and found homes for them, including ours. I had committed an act which had consequences that I could not foresee, and for which there was no justification. I was, after all, the site manager, the person who was supposed to know what he was doing, the self-appointed minor monarch of my small preserve – yet with a single callous act, I had created a litter of helpless orphans who now had to fend for themselves or perish.

The fact is my ducks were not in danger from cats or anything else. They were secure inside their wire compound – that is, until they learned how to fly – because it was high enough and strong enough to discourage any predators. There was certainly no attack in progress, probably none being contemplated, and no evidence that the cat had been the culprit when one of the ducks had previously gone missing. She was just doing what I learned much later all cats do – watching, observing detail, noticing movement - behaviors that I often displayed myself at the battlefield but which I did not recognize in another creature.

I had prided myself on making rational decisions, the right choice for the right reasons, and measuring up to my own self-imposed and impossible standards. Now I had done something cruel and done it with indifference to the pain and suffering I'd caused. What gave me the right to interfere with nature – a cat watching a flock of nearly grown ducks who would have been more than a match for a single feline? And what gave me the right to exert control where none was needed – to take a life that had done no harm to me and, in any case, was not mine to take?

One never knows where a decision may lead, what doubts may arise about one's own judgment and ability, or how easily one can overreact to a given situation. There may have been reasons for what I did, but these were explanations, not excuses or substitutes for personal accountability. I had grown up in Florida around guns; my father had several in the house. He was not a hunter but was always swapping and trading firearms, though I suspect that he was more interested in the bartering process than the result; once, when he was part owner of a filling station, my father traded five gallons of gas for an *owl* - not because he had any particular affinity for wildlife, but because it was unusual. The owl was certainly that.

Firearms, however, tended to be his area of interest, and with the weapons he'd acquired, he and I and my brother would go off on many a weekend to a makeshift target range in a secluded area in the nearby Everglades and shoot at objects we'd bring from home. Being environmentally oblivious as was the custom of that time, we'd always leave behind a trail of punctured cans and shattered bottles, the debris of our day's

35

outing. I'm also sorry to say that, in any of the various canals which crisscrossed that natural wilderness so close to our home, an occasional waterborne creature might also have been a target as well.

As an adolescent boy, I was taught weapons safety by my Dad. I knew enough not to assume that a firearm was loaded until you checked to make sure it wasn't. I also knew that you should never point a gun – loaded or not - at anyone, and that there would be consequences, legal or otherwise, if you shot a person, but not if you shot an animal unless a human owner was involved. I learned the difference between a revolver, a semi-automatic handgun, and an automatic rifle. I knew how to take them apart and clean them, making sure, of course, that they were empty first, and I liked the sound of their names – Winchester, Colt, Smith and Wesson, Remington, all conjuring up romantic images of the Old West; Luger, Beretta, Walther, and Weatherby, suggesting the intrigue and mystery of distant European countries.

The craftsmanship of firearms interested me too – all those finely machined parts working in precise unison to release a tremendous force from a small, brass capsule. I liked the smell of gun oil and cordite, and the heft of metal in my hands, but above all, I liked the sound of firearms – it was fun to pull a trigger and make a loud noise that made the weapon jump and sometimes those around me as well. It was also a way of releasing steam and expressing frustration over the implicit lack of control in my own teenage life. I was dimly aware that while adults held sway over me as they would any kid, 1 could be their equal or better with a weapon. I also knew that being armed attracted attention and added to one's sense of importance. I was too immature at the time, however, to know that what I was wielding was nothing less than the power of life and death, and it was that power which subconsciously appealed to me.

My exposure to guns, however, did not include instruction about the harm they could do. I knew, of course, that they could kill or hurt people, but that always seemed to happen in a painless sort of way. This misconception was easy to believe in the 1950s when I was growing up because of all the bloodless episodes that appeared on television and in film. Guns were depicted as the solution to problems, and when they were used to right a wrong, the villains fell cleanly to the floor as if they had fainted. Occasionally, there were dramatic pratfalls involved in the demise of the bad guy, but there appeared to be no suffering at all. A trigger was pulled, a shot was fired, a problem was solved. It all seemed very simple.

When, as a boy and later in life, I pulled a trigger and fired a shot, I gave no thought to the physical damage that I could cause by sending a high-speed projectile through flesh and tissue, killing or seriously wounding any animal in my sights. In my mind, there was no relationship between cause and effect. A vital link had gone missing; it was as if the mechanical operation of a car had been explained and demonstrated to me without mentioning that vehicles were meant to be driven. That fundamental omission had been reinforced by hours of exposure to the media of the day and the absence of another crucial fact from my informal firearms training: the realization that the ultimate purpose of any firearm is to end life, and that's exactly what it would do if a living creature was the target – and when that happened, it wouldn't be like the movies.

This mindset, learned at an early age, created a separation between one event and another – the pull of a trigger and the death of an animal. Another factor was my indifference toward animals in general. There were, of course, animals in my family's house when I was growing up as there are in most houses, and they covered quite a range of species from the aforementioned owl, to monkeys – this was 1950's Florida, don't forget - and snakes, the last of which were kept in boxes and small cages and then placed in the laundry room where my mother inevitably came upon them on wash day, much to her chagrin and no doubt to her terror. Tantalizing as speculation about them might be, my father's reasons for repeatedly putting snakes where he must have known my Mother would find them are, unfortunately, a whole other story, one that is well beyond the scope of this narrative. Happily, the snakes were soon transported elsewhere, but their impact in my home was, shall we say, memorable. With the exception of these slithery creatures which he "collected" himself, all the other animals were probably gotten in trade because my Dad didn't care what he got in return so long as it was unusual and he'd gotten the best of the deal. In fact, that seemed to be the whole point.

Though we never had a cat, we had several dogs, but there was never a strong bond between any of them and us. I don't remember playing with these dogs, and I don't recall that they had any active role in household. They did not seem very important; having been there for as long as anyone could remember, they generally went unnoticed, like a piece of old furniture. Why have a pet at all then, one might ask? Perhaps because some people think they are supposed to. It doesn't mean you have to play with the animal or spend time with it or relate to it in any meaningful way or care about it, so long as it's provided with food and shelter. If it's a dog, you might simply tie it up outside and leave it there. If it's a cat, you might let it out on its own, possibly to wander off, to be exposed to all kinds of hazards ranging from being hit by a car to being attacked by a wild animal. In either situation, the pet that was brought into the home – ours or anyone else's - was subject to whatever we humans meted out to it, whether it be kindness or cruelty, or perhaps even worse, indifference.

I learned early that, when it came to cats and dogs, there was a double standard, with felines viewed more negatively. Through legend and folklore, they were associated with superstition and the so-called black arts. They were supposedly aloof, solitary, and unfriendly, not as affectionate as dogs. Their perceived independence or detachment – perhaps even their seeming resistance to human company - could well create resentment among some people, causing them to feel that cats, being less sociable, could be left alone more often, and fend for themselves.

Because we didn't have a cat in my house when I was growing up, it was easy for me to believe in that stereotype. Though I discovered as I got older that generalities are often disproved when personal knowledge replaces hearsay, misconceptions about felines continued into my adult life, and I unconsciously applied the double standard I'd grown up with. If it had been a dog I'd seen that day by my ducks, I wouldn't have shot it; I'd have chased it off and tried to find its owner. It never occurred to me to do that with a cat.

In the environment in which I was raised, it was a shock to me that anyone could feel strong emotions toward a pet. That changed one day when I came home from junior high school, and noticed a blanket spread out in our carport. Under it was the body of our dog Mike. My initial reaction was simple and direct: Mike had been alive when I'd left that morning; now he wasn't. It was my first experience with death. That realization was followed by a natural curiosity – I wondered what had happened - and I started toward the front door when I heard my mother crying. I had never heard her cry before, in any situation, and now she was weeping for poor Mike, who'd been run over by a car. Even as a teenage boy, I was affected by something unusual, something I knew you didn't see every day; an adult upset enough to shed tears, and not knowing (or caring) who was there to see or hear. My mother's grief was real and unforced and, in my family, unique. It made an impression that lasts to this day.

Unfortunately, it was only an impression, and didn't extend to other parts of my life or translate into action. Over time, I began to suspect that some adults felt strongly about animals, but I didn't understand that animals experience nearly the same range of emotions as we do; though our actions often suggest otherwise, humans have no monopoly on pain, fear, affection, happiness, despair, grief, sadness or loss.

I must have thought – if I thought about it at all – that in some irrational way, cats didn't experience any of these feelings. Out of that ignorance, I had done something that could never be changed or erased, and, as a result, had created what I began to see as a cosmic debt, one that could only paid to Cato himself. Though Page and I had grown to love him, I was also motivated by a strong sense of obligation to keep Cato safe and well and happy. After all, it was through my actions, deeply rooted in the origins of indifference, that he'd been orphaned. I could not change what I'd done, but I could still do my very best for him. He would never be hungry, he would never be hurt, and he would never again be abandoned. I would see to that for as long as he was with us.

I was trying to live up to what I perceived as Cato's unspoken expectations, and it wasn't always easy. My ethical compass had pointed me in the wrong direction and needed some serious recalibration. I hadn't known or had forgotten a basic truth – just as a pebble thrown into a pond creates ripples, an act has the same effect, and the consequences which result, may not be apparent or predictable.

No matter what appears to be the case at the time, there is a relationship between events; nothing is isolated or exists by itself in a vacuum. Therefore, unless one knew or could know in advance what the consequences of any given action would be and was prepared to accept those consequences, then the act itself should be reconsidered and possibly not committed at all. It was clear that my upbringing, my background and education were devoid of a vital element: I had no sense of the value of life except my own. Abstractly, of course, I 'd agree, as we all would, that life is important, but it's the practice, not the theory, that counts. I had a moral blind spot, a myopia focused almost exclusively on my own self-interest.

Cato would help improve my vision. I had learned from books, and I had learned from experience (though not nearly as much as I should have), but I had never before learned from an animal. Animals as mentors and guides, of course, are nothing new. As the saying goes, let me be the person my cat thinks I am. Like many light-hearted comments, that remark hints at a serious truth. One learns about life by living and witnessing life, and there's no better example of life than the exuberance, the exhilaration, the dynamic energy of a kitten whose sheer joy and playful antics can brighten the darkest cast of mind. One also learns to trust by being trusted, and there's no relationship quite like the one created by the faith that an animal shows when, though it knows that you have the potential to do it harm, you will care for it and protect it instead. And unlike the uneven course of many human relationships, animals remind us every day that one learns about love simply by being loved.

Animals can also demonstrate, as Cato did for me, that different levels of perception and reality often go unnoticed in everyday life. It's fairly well known, for example, that animals can perceive the approach of earthquakes and tsunamis long before these natural disasters strike. Happily, Cato never had the opportunity to display his skill in this area, but he could easily reflect the feelings of the people around him. If I was upset or happy or tense, it was somehow communicated to him. I stopped taking Cato to the local veterinarian because it made me nervous, which, in turn, made *him* nervous. Page, who was much less anxious in these situations, took over, and Cato settled down. She was calm, and so was he.

Cato could also sense danger long before it sensed him. On several occasions, he would suddenly snap to his alarm mode – posture rigid, body made as small as possible, mental antennae on full alert – and, noticing something that I could neither see nor hear, quickly move to a safe location, one that also had an exit just in case. A few seconds or minutes later, a dog or a raccoon or some other unexpected creature came into view – unexpected, that is, by me, at least until I realized – and appreciated – the special perceptions that Cato had and which I obviously lacked. We've all heard about dogs who somehow know when their masters will come home, and wait by the door a half-hour before they arrive. Cats also have a whole level of what might be described as intuitive knowledge, a connection to the natural world that is not fully understood, and which, while it may not be beyond us, we seldom recognize or use.

Cato was also teaching me that though realities can overlap, they are multiple and that there was more than one way to perceive the world and respond to it. It was all part of the time – and there was a great deal of it – we spent together at Stony Point that was marked by the shared pleasure of very good friends. Though I still felt an obligation toward this creature whose fate was now linked to my own, I enjoyed his quiet company, his studied elegance, the gentle brush against the leg that said "I'm here," but I also felt more aware than ever of having destroyed a life to bring his life into mine.

6

A Magical Time

Along with the rest of the staff at Stony Point, I worked every weekend and holiday each year from mid-April to the end of October when the battlefield closed for the season, not only to avoid the appearance of a double standard but also because we were too shorthanded to do otherwise. Besides, it was virtually impossible to separate myself from the workplace when I lived in the middle of it. If I wanted to get distance from the countless tasks that needed to be done, even on days when the site was closed, I had to leave the premises and go somewhere else for a few hours. However, as conscientious (or obsessive) as I was, it was sometimes difficult to do even that.

Like any job, being site manager had its good and bad points. When I had the time – which wasn't often – I was able to do some research which yielded some positive results. One winter, I learned about an 18th century map at the Pennsylvania Historical Society in Philadelphia and drove down to see it. To my surprise, it proved to be drawn by Captain William Marshall, a British engineer who had been taken captive at Stony Point and confined near Lancaster, Pennsylvania, not far from where his map was now located. Needless to say, this discovery - more than two hundred years after the battle – was not only very unexpected but also provided new information about the British defenses, all from a previously unknown contemporary source.

Another important discovery occurred when I'd heard that the transcript of the court-martial of Lieutenant Colonel Henry Johnson, the British commander at Stony Point, was available from the Public Records Office in London. I arranged to obtain a photocopy, and there, written in an 18th- century hand, were the exact proceedings of the Colonel's trial. To my delight, the chief witness proved to be none other than the same Captain Marshall who had drawn the map found in Pennsylvania. His testimony imparted more new light from the past, and helped explain what had happened and why during the battle fought so many years before.

I also developed educational programs at Stony Point because when I arrived in 1992, there were only two annual events: a daytime battle re-enactment and a Halloween extravaganza, complete with stuffed, life-size dummies. Re-enacting the battle, of course, was neither possible nor safe. After all, when the Americans stormed the British defenses at night in 1779, most of them had waded through the shallow waters of Haverstraw Bay and were armed only with unloaded muskets and fixed bayonets. I'd also believed for some time that so-called "re-enactments" were misleading because despite the most painstaking research, inaccuracies were bound to creep in, simply because records of historic events are seldom, if ever, complete. When such vacuums occurred, the temptation was to fill them, even with something that was unsupported by the facts. My solution was to continue to hold the daytime event, call it a "commemoration" – a more accurate term, in any case - and explain, through narration, that the re-enactors were demonstrating military weapons and tactics of the period, not attempting to re-create the actual battle itself.

45

The Halloween program, needless to say, had nothing to do with the battle itself (which was fought in July, remember) or with any other part of the site's history. One of my first actions therefore as site manager was to cancel that event because keeping the Halloween program in place would have implied that Stony Point's real history was of no interest. The Halloween program, however, had been popular, so I knew that site-related programs had to be created to fill the void. I also knew that the story of the battle and the lighthouse could be more engaging and inspiring than any made-up tale about ghosts and pumpkins. If I didn't believe that, I shouldn't be site manager. I soon set to work.

The first task required a combination of physical dexterity and no small amount of energy: moving the Halloween dummies. There were many of them, and they were being stored in the site house where Page and I would soon be living, and which had been unoccupied for some time. We were greatly outnumbered by these bulky manikins who had claimed the unyielding right of possession. Stacked on the upper floor where we would have our bedroom, they were very large and very much in the way. We had just arrived, and we were not about to share our new digs with a crowd of permanent houseguests, inert though they may be. They were soon hauled off, and the house was ours and ours alone.

Next, my attention was directed toward the creation of new programs, including daily musket and artillery demonstrations, as well as walking tours I discovered that if the word "walking" was substituted for "guided," visitors were far more likely to be interested, even though it was the same experience. Not for the first time, I learned the power of language, and that what something was called could make all the difference.

I also designed special events that, unlike the Halloween program, had some relationship with the site's history. For example, when the battle of Stony Point was fought in July 1779, two companies of the 71st Highland Regiment were part of the British garrison, and bagpipers had long been an established part of Scottish military tradition. That fact suggested to me that an annual special event featuring a pipe and drum band would not only be entertaining but also appropriate.

In addition, I led battlefield evening tours, which consisted of a lantern walk through the grounds, where we met actors hired to play the parts of some of the original British soldiers at Stony Point. Afterwards, visitors participated in a re-creation of the court-martial of Lieutenant Colonel Henry Johnson, who had been captured at battle's end. Because I had obtained a copy of Johnson's 1781 trial, we had a totally authentic script. We knew exactly who said what, where they were during the battle, and in many cases, what had happened to them afterwards at war's end. Nothing was invented. It was fun, it was exciting, it was history at its best.

School tours were frequently offered as well, my favorite being a program called "Outpost on the Hudson." For approximately three hours, a class of fourth or fifth graders learned to march and drill, gather wood and haul water, and, under staff supervision, prepare a hot meal over a fire – in short, to accomplish many of the mundane tasks that fell to an 18th century soldier. By the end of the program, any romantic notions about the glamour of military life had been replaced by a healthy respect for the rigors that such a life actually demanded. It was a lot of work but the kids accomplished a great deal and had a lot of fun doing it. Among other things, they learned to cooperate with each other and be responsible for their own behavior – values that were applicable to civilian life as well. As they formed two columns to leave and head back to school, I'd end the program with two final questions; how many people were glad they were no longer soldiers, and how many people were also glad I was not their teacher? The vote was always unanimous. Thankful that they were just kids again, and that I would not hold sway in their classroom, they marched off, ready to rejoin the 20th century.

These programs were very satisfying and very intensive, but even when no programs or tours were scheduled, I was mostly outdoors, working with staff, talking to visitors, responding to questions about the battle or the lighthouse, and in general keeping an eye on the entire property. By five in the afternoon, visitors had left, the staff had gone, the gate was closed, and it would be another two hours before Page returned home. No matter how good a day I'd had, it was always better with Cato, and it was during this brief window of time that I probably enjoyed him the most.

Our conversations occurred without the formality of words, which was fine with me - I'd been using words all day and was glad to get away from them. I'd pet him and he'd let me close my hand gently around his face and stroke his ears. Then we might sit on adjoining rockers on the deck or the front porch and enjoy what had been a public place, but was now once again our private preserve – at least until the battlefield opened next morning.

Sometimes, we might simply stroll through the backyard, head up the hill where the museum and lighthouse were located, or walk along the south side of the peninsula, low to the water, and see the marinas close by, buzzing with the activity of sail and powerboats leaving or entering port. Cato, of course, had a tendency to get distracted by a bird, a sudden movement in the brush, or a squirrel scampering to a safe perch. That was fine with me. I was in no hurry. I had been in a hurry all day; now I had a chance to adopt Cato's pace which was unforced, perfectly natural, and directed only by whatever unforeseen opportunities presented themselves. Humans might focus on a destination; a feline knew that the destination was incidental to the walk itself. It was just one more perspective from what I used to consider an unlikely source.

My favorite special event was the lighthouse evening tour in which I played a relatively minor role. The tour began in the museum where a slide show was presented that documented the history of the lighthouse. Then I led the audience along the path illuminated by candles to the lighthouse where staff was waiting at the entrance and up in the lantern room where the light could be seen, flashing at regular intervals through the darkness.

As visitors waited their turn to ascend to the top of the lighthouse, they enjoyed the ambiance of the Hudson River, seen at night from one of the highest points on the peninsula. Because modern intrusions were almost totally concealed, the atmosphere was conducive to imagination, and many who were there could easily envisage the light keepers at work, performing their lonely vigils, warning vessels to stay clear - keeping watch, as it were, over the lives of others. It was a magical time. Exciting as the tour was, it couldn't have happened unless the lighthouse had been restored and reopened, but that's a whole story in itself.

7

Keeping the Promise

When I arrived on the scene, the Stony Point lighthouse had been closed since 1925 when it was decommissioned and light keeping operations were moved down to the tip of the peninsula by the water's edge. The lighthouse exterior had been restored in 1986, and the light tower itself was intact but abandoned and empty: the building had been gutted and all the interior equipment, including the lens, had been removed. The lighthouse remained a potential target for vandals and a forlorn shadow of its former self. It needed to be restored, reopened, and re-lighted.

Despite the local control and autonomy I enjoyed as site manager, this was not a project I could undertake alone. Financial and logistical support would have to come from other sources, and it would not be easy. Though the Stony Point lighthouse was the first and the oldest on the Hudson and one of the few owned by New York State, my request for assistance would be only one among many that were received every year from all the other parks and historic sites that the state administered. I knew as well that the restoration project would continue to be stalled (as it had been thus far) unless a lens – the optical heart of any lighthouse – could be located.

For some months, I searched diligently for the lighthouse's 1902 Fresnel lens, so named for its inventor, Augustin Fresnel, but without success. I then went to plan "B"; if I couldn't locate the original lens, perhaps I could find one made during the same period and of the same "order," Fresnel's term for size and intensity. More research led me to the Hudson River Maritime Museum in Kingston, New York, where I spied just the lens I was looking for. The museum director would loan us the lens, if the Coast Guard, who had loaned it to them, would give their consent. I contacted them, and they readily agreed.

The lens, of course, is at the top of any lighthouse – which means you have to be able to get the top to begin with. There was no floor in the Stony Point lighthouse, either at ground level or higher up where the lens would be, in what was called the lantern room. There were no stairs either. All of this had to be designed and built according to original specifications, and all of it had to be in place before the lens arrived. It was a powerful incentive to complete the work as soon as possible; equally important, however, was the unflagging support provided by Bob Binnewies, Executive Director of the Palisades Interstate Park Commission, whose belief in the project went far to assure its success.

By the fall of 1995, the restoration, brought about by many talented individuals working together, was nearly complete, and the lens had been transferred to us, delivered to the battlefield and installed with the assistance of Coast Guard personnel. Dedication day was set for October 7.

A ceremony was planned, speeches were written, state officials would be present, and someone would have to perform the symbolic act of turning on the light for the first time since 1926, in effect giving life back to the lighthouse. I felt strongly that whoever it was should have a personal link to those keepers who had served so long and well for nearly a century. I found exactly the right person. Millard Heaphy, the nephew of the last keeper, had worked with his uncle at the lighthouse, and was still alive, though in his mid-eighties and confined to a wheelchair. I asked him if he would be willing to help us, and he agreed.

It was nearly dusk, and the day itself was overcast, but a crowd had gathered for the occasion. After the usual introductory remarks and comments, I turned to Mr. Heaphy and asked him to give a prearranged signal to one of our staff at the top of the lighthouse to turn on the light. In a few seconds, for the first time in nearly seventy years, the old beacon flashed its beam across the Hudson in the distance and the lighthouse was officially re-opened.

Preventing a vital part of history from decay and preserving it for the future is a little like throwing a lifeline to a person in distress, someone who would perish unless a rescue attempt succeeded. That feeling, combined with the intense satisfaction of helping to re-create something from its component parts and making it work again after so many years of neglect and decline, lead to an indescribable sense of accomplishment. For me, the lighthouse was not just a structure; it was also a tribute to the men and women who had illuminated the darkness for nearly a hundred years, faithfully protecting countless strangers from the hazards and dangers of the unpredictable Hudson. Commemorating that tradition was among the most rewarding experiences for me at Stony Point, and to this day I regard it as the high point of my career.

The satisfaction derived from successful programs and projects was offset by the part of my job I liked least – being responsible for security, particularly after hours. The museum was equipped with both intrusion and fire alarms, both of which tended to go off at the most inconvenient times, usually in the wee hours of the morning. If I didn't actually hear them – the site house was only a few hundred yards away – I would get a phone call from the park police who had been informed by the security monitoring company that one of the two alarms had sounded. I had the key to the museum and was the only one who knew the access code, so I had to get out of bed, throw on some clothes, and rush up the hill to the museum – all this, mind you, at 2 AM or so, and in all kinds of weather, including rain and snow – and wait for the police or the fire trucks to arrive. There was never a break in or fire, but that wasn't evident at the time, and each alarm had to be taken seriously. In all instances – and there were many of them over the nearly eight and half years I was manager – the system had malfunctioned because of age, or because someone forgot to secure a door, or perhaps a sensor had worn out. Needless to say, it all made for many a sleepless night.

Looking back now, the only time the site was in any real jeopardy occurred when a train derailed nearby. It should be explained at this point that an active freight line ran north and south through the battlefield peninsula beyond the front gate and just below the site house. These trains came and went at all hours and were an endless source of noise, smoke and pollution.

One year, just prior to the annual commemoration of the battle in July, a train jumped the tracks north of the battlefield, and some of the cars contained hazardous materials. When the wreck occurred around four in the morning, I heard a resounding crash, which was soon followed by the arrival of police cars, fire trucks and other official vehicles – along with the inevitable reporters – all of whom began to descend en masse on the site and along the tracks.

Even though I was on the spot, I was among the least informed. At first, the possibility of hazardous materials spilled close by had not been revealed by those in charge, but soon it became evident that the threat of contamination was real. For the first time in memory, the battlefield was shut down, the annual commemoration activities were cancelled, the staff sent home, and Page and I, along with Cato, were told to leave the premises until it was safe to come back. Luckily for us, that was sooner than we expected, and we were able to return that evening. Up till that point, I'd known that the trains were a nuisance, but I'd never thought they could also be dangerous. Why they were carrying hazardous materials through one of the busiest, most heavily populated corridors of the state – along the lower Hudson River valley north to Albany - is still a mystery to me.

Managing Stony Point Battlefield had its lighter moments as well. Though I was usually knowledgeable about the site's history and glib in my responses, occasionally a question would arise for which I had no answer. One day a visitor asked, without any touch of sarcasm, why so many battles were fought in state and national parks. That one stymied me at first - but then the advantages became obvious – plenty of free parking, access to public restrooms, and the use of picnic tables for lunch. So long as chronology wasn't important, and it didn't matter what happened first – that is, if you forgot that the battle came before the park - it made a lot of sense.

Once when I was stationed near the entrance at closing time to discourage vehicles from proceeding any further, a very well-dressed woman - – possibly lost but clearly on the way to somewhere else – pulled up in a very expensive car. The whirr of an electric motor accompanied the lowering of a darkly tinted driver's side window, and I politely told her we'd be closing in a few minutes and that she could turn around in the circle a few feet ahead. The window went up, and she went off, following my directions. When she returned, the car stopped, and again the tinted window was lowered. "What happened here?" she asked. Sensing that a short reply was more appropriate than a longer, more detailed one, I said, " There was a battle between the British and the Americans." "Who won?" she inquired. " The Americans." I answered. "I'm so glad" she gushed, as the window whirred up and the car drove off. It was a complete Stony Point experience.

Another time, the road in front of the site house was being paved, and the foreman and I were watching his crew at work. He described other projects they had completed, and though things were progressing nicely as we spoke, he referred to them as "jug heads." I wondered aloud why he used such an unflattering term. Just at that moment, a small roller approached to smooth the newly-paved driveway; a nearby workman tossed a large ring of keys to the operator, but he fumbled the catch, and the keys fell in front of the moving machine, to be crushed and imbedded forever in the sticky, black tar. The timing couldn't have been better. "See what I mean?" said the foreman.

Throughout all that had happened at the battlefield, I was conscious of being part of a tradition at Stony Point, not only that of the light keepers who had steadfastly guided mariners for nearly a hundred years, but also the one set by William and Sarah Ten Eyck, the first keepers of the battlefield, who, between them, served a total of 41 years, from 1903 to 1944.

I could not, of course, expect to equal the tenure of these exceptional individuals, but I was determined to equal their dedication. To me, the title "site manager" sounded too bland and bureaucratic. The word "keeper" was a far better choice to describe what I promised myself I would do: keep the story of the battle and the lighthouse alive; keep the battlefield protected and preserved; keep its identity intact so it would not be minimized and changed by those who thought of it as just another park.

The Marshall map, interpretive demonstrations, special events, guided tours, evening programs, new research about the battle – I felt I'd achieved a great deal in a relatively short time. Adults and children alike had been engaged on a number of personal levels, with the result that the story of the battle and the lighthouse had begun to be exciting, relevant and real. Other improvements, of course, could always be made to the battlefield, but perhaps I had done all I could do and it was time to consider a change. It was not an easy thought.

Often, at day's end, having returned with Cato from an early evening stroll, Page and I would sit with him on the covered porch of our house, basking in the quiet, natural setting that encompassed us, and enjoying each other's company while the sun set over the nearby river. As the fading light signaled the approach of night, I'd consider how fortunate we were to have had the privilege of living in such a wonderful and remarkable place, and I would also think how difficult it would be to leave.

Now, the lighthouse once again cast its beam across the waters, and the sounds of battle – two armies clashing by night - had long since faded. Throughout the changing seasons and the passing years – from the stark outlines of winter to the brilliant array of fall colors – Stony Point Battlefield was slowly returning to its original pastoral setting, re-establishing the rule of nature over the temporary effect and influence of human affairs. A place of conflict, turmoil and sacrifice was being restored to the intrinsic beauty of a pristine landscape, creating both a gateway to the historic past and a place for quiet reflection.

By taking care of the battlefield and contributing to its preservation, I felt that my stewardship had been a positive one which would now form a small part of the site's legacy and its continuing transition to the future. This unique historic property had not been mine, and never could be, but in some way it would always be an integral part of who I was.

8

A Special Part of the Globe

By December 2000, I felt it was time to leave. Whatever I'd accomplished had come at a high price, one I could no longer afford to pay. I was emotionally and physically drained from the burden of constantly needing to demonstrate my competence and abilities while striving to improve the battlefield in every way I could. I was too demanding of myself and others; where I should have been flexible, I was too often rigid and dogmatic. If I wasn't working, I was thinking about working, and it wasn't just work anymore; it was how I defined myself. After more than eight years, I was still trying too hard to show what I could do, and I was tired – too tired to muster the zeal and drive to get things done, too impatient with those whose support was necessary to accomplish other tasks I considered vital for the site. Yet without the constant effort I'd expended over the years, far less progress would have been made. I had what someone has charitably described as "the virtues of my defects," but it simply could not continue.

In January 2001, we relocated to the quiet town of Bristol, in midcoast Maine, and The Whisker Club established a New England branch. It was a decision that proved to be more unsettling than we'd anticipated, because in leaving our state, our home, and my employment, we'd made dramatic changes on several levels that required much more adjustment than we would have thought as we tried to adapt to our new life.

It began by the move itself, which, as everyone knows, is almost always disruptive and produces great stress and anxiety. One reason why is that taking all the physical things we own and putting them in another house or apartment is a little like uprooting them, and since we are at least in part defined by what we possess, that makes us feel uprooted as well.

We also discovered that our furniture in transit went through a change of its own: it tended to increase in size, with the result that when the sofa or the chairs or the bed or the tables were placed in our new home, they seemed much bigger than they were before, and what had appeared to be a very ample floor plan now looked very crowded and much smaller. It's a phenomenon that's probably all too familiar.

Then, of course, there was the arduous and seemingly endless process of unpacking and putting all that stuff where we wanted it to be. That took a lot of time. By early spring, however, we were feeling fairly situated, and I began to turn my attention to the great outdoors, planting saplings and bushes and getting the lawn to grow. Our house was new, but sat amid a scarred landscape of destruction: gouged earth, cut trees, wide expanses of brown where there had been green – in short, a typical construction site. I wanted our surroundings to recover as soon as possible, so I focused on replacing desolation with the new life of verdant foliage. The contractor had seeded the area and covered it with straw, and for a while grass was beginning to sprout, but that drastically changed when it was learned that the covering straw had also introduced army worms. Frankly, we weren't ready for company of any sort, least of all the uninvited kind, the type that would literally devour nearly any vegetation in sight.

In no time at all, these voracious predators feasted on my budding grass. Their appetite was insatiable; day and night, these writhing masses of striped insects ate away, like creatures from a horror movie. Not only could they be seen; they could also be heard, emitting a continuous, monotonous drone. Short of using potentially dangerous chemicals, there was no way to discourage them. They would stop on their own when there was no longer anything to eat, in the manner of houseguests who leave when the food runs out, and that's exactly what happened.

The new lawn was just a memory; now it was more like a desert. A local landscaper dropped by to assess the damage. The grass wasn't actually dead, he said, it had just been given a really close haircut. Neighbors thought it was drought, but it couldn't be that because we'd had plenty of rain. It was army worms, and ours was the only lawn in the area that they had chosen to visit, no doubt because of the contaminated straw. Lucky us, I thought. It was nice to be special, but couldn't it have been in some other way?

I replanted and revived the lawn, and after much time and effort, it began to recover and even flourish. In a way, I almost didn't mind because it kept me busy. Besides, as anyone can tell you, in a new home there's always something to do. That was a welcome prospect because I now had plenty of time and very few obligations. The real problem, however, was that I had long ago crossed the line between what I did and who I was. They were now one and the same, and separating them would not be easy. The time, thought and energy I'd used to manage Stony Point Battlefield would have to be redirected and used instead to manage my own life. Now, seven years later, it is still a work in progress, an identity still in the making.

Cato, of course, came with us when we moved. He was a family member, after all, and we'd no sooner leave him behind than we'd leave a child. When the house we had built was ready for us, we introduced him to his new home. We knew that cats were very sensitive to changes in environment, but much of our furniture was familiar to Cato, and his natural curiosity soon led him to explore every nook and cranny – especially the small, dark spaces under the stairs and in the corners, as well as the many closets and the extra large basement in which to conduct his regular patrols and claim these new places as his own. Though he had his own cat door as he did at Stony Point and could come and go as he chose, he'd usually prefer that we open the regular or "people" door for him. Just as many of us humans would, he enjoyed the attention.

At Cato's suggestion, we also installed a "Cat Crossing" sign near our driveway to warn passing motorists that a new feline had arrived and was now living in the neighborhood. Though we had moved many miles to a different place and a new life, Cato was assured, at some very basic level, that we were still together and all would be well. No matter where we were, we'd always be a family, perhaps not in the conventional sense, but a family nonetheless.

At first, we were concerned with predators in our neighborhood, but Cato soon proved by the occasional "gifts" he presented to us that he was at the top of the local food chain. Nonetheless, he was appropriately wary, and when a young fisher came on the property, Cato spotted him long before I did, and headed for cover. Our house has a cathedral ceiling and, appropriately enough, a cat walk leading to a beam on the second floor. That beam was the ultimate refuge from anything Cato didn't like; he'd learned a long time ago that prudence was the better part of valor, and his presence there was a sure sign that there was some critter in the great outdoors that he wanted no part of.

As in the past, Cato's perceptions were more acute than mine, probably better than most humans. By a superior sense of smell and sound and perhaps a whole extra dimension of sensitivity to danger, he knew long before I did that it was time to retreat. It was a natural ability I always admired and envied, largely because I didn't have it and probably never could. Because of his acute awareness, I learned to trust Cato to be safe when he was outside, though I still occasionally worried about his location and when he'd be coming home. That was just my irrational anxiety being projected onto him; nonetheless, it was always reassuring to hear the flap of his cat door open, signaling his arrival.

Cato adjusted to his new role as a Maine pussycat. He came and went through the night, and if he was hungry in the wee hours, he would ascend the stairs to our bedroom and nudge one of us – usually Page – on her elbow to say, "I'm hungry – feed me." If that approach proved ineffective, a feline-to-human nose rub was lovingly but firmly offered as a gentle call for action.

However, if Page was still too slow to respond, Cato might jump up and land somewhere on her torso, a tactic which invariably got her attention and produced the intended result, though not without some occasional (and very understandable) grumpiness on her part. I always thought these antics were amusing, but then again I was the observer, not the recipient of Cato's persistent efforts.

Sometimes at night when he'd come in just to say "hello," we'd tent our blankets and he'd crawl under them or he would nestle between us and nap. I would picture the three of us together in the deep dark of the early hours or the half light of the approaching dawn and think how fortunate we all were to have found each other, lying here in a safe, warm place, sharing not only each other's lives but also a common bond of love and kinship. And I could envision the stars and the crescent moon looking down through the skylight above our bed at a scene of utter peace – three creatures snuggled together in the complete comfort and trust of contented sleep. I was never happier.

In winter, when there was snow on the ground, I always cleared a path for Cato around our house, either by hand or with the snow blower so there'd be a circuit that he could patrol from one outside door to another. After all, we needed a path to get around– why wouldn't he? It was Cato's territory as well as ours, and I suspect he defined himself in part, as we did ourselves, in terms of his physical place in the world, his own special part of the globe.

I also adjusted, or tried to adjust, to my new role as a retired person – a misnomer if I ever heard one. While

64

it was true that I didn't have to go to an office anymore or work a particular schedule, I was as busy as ever, settling into our new home and tackling countless projects that I'd never been able to get to before. One was publishing the first comprehensive account of the battle of Stony Point in more than a hundred years, based on research and primary sources - information that I no longer used on a daily basis but which I still retained. Telling the story of the battle in print – something I'd been doing verbally for years – was a way of hopefully consigning it to the past – my past. With projects like this and others, I soon wondered how I ever had time for a full-time job. I've since learned that's a fairly common experience.

We also had more time to travel. As we'd always done before, whenever we left town, we had someone come to our house and stay over to take care of Cato. We'd produce copiously detailed instructions about his food, his activities and playthings, his possible locations, and his schedule, which was, of course, always subject to a re-ordering of feline priorities. All these details must have seemed intimidating and perhaps unnecessary to some, particularly those who felt that animals were, after all, only animals.

By contrast, we felt we were just being conscientious by providing complete instructions, including contact information, in anticipation of any contingency that might arise in our absence. No doubt I was more obsessive than Page – I often wished I could talk to Cato on the phone when we were away – but that was because I could never forget how and why he came to us. Clearly, we didn't distinguish between cat and human, denoting the former to a lesser category of importance;

we were responsible for him, we had bonded to him, he was a part of us. It was that simple. Page and I had decided not to have a human family, so Cato, in effect, was our only child – that is until something happened that we never expected, shattering the harmony we'd come to enjoy but should have known would never last.

9

A Decline in Tranquility

Most people would probably agree that we humans are considerably less than perfect. We don't always do the right thing, we tend to be self-centered and self-indulgent, and many of us subscribe to faulty standards of success, often measuring ourselves by what we own rather than by what we give. We usually have far more than we need, and we have a tendency to keep it. Sometimes, we also impose our will on others, achieving a result that is just the opposite of what we'd intended.

In July 2005, I heard a series of plaintive, cat-like sounds outside our bedroom window in the wee hours of the morning. At first, I thought it must be Cato, but he had come inside. I went out to investigate, and saw a pair of eyes glinting in the darkness. The eyes also saw me, and disappeared into the surrounding woods. The animal returned several times on several different nights. It was a stray cat, and it was friendly, so I was able to approach it. It wore a flea collar, and hopefully had an owner somewhere. I placed a sign in the local post office and conducted an extensive door-to-door canvass of neighbors, but the results were negative: no one claimed our feline visitor. I even got close enough to tuck a small, handwritten note under the cat's collar, thinking its owner would retrieve it when the cat returned home. The next night, the cat appeared once again below our bedroom window with the note still under the collar where I'd placed it.

Apparently, the cat had been left on our road by someone who thought that it was morally acceptable to discard a helpless creature, dumping it like yesterday's garbage after inviting it home. According to the local animal control officer, that scenario happened all too often. Meanwhile, Cato, our own resident cat and longtime companion, was not pleased about the occasional drop-by company, especially because, as it later turned out, the visitor whose yowls signaled his early morning presence was an un-neutered male. Not only had the new cat been abandoned - his owner hadn't been responsible enough to have him fixed.

Our cat was not happy about sharing his territory, and we were not happy about leaving the new cat to his own devices in the woods, fearing that sooner or later, he would fall victim to accident, disease or predators, so we called the local animal shelter, not really knowing what to expect. One of the staff responded to our concerns in a sympathetic, understanding manner, especially when we expressed misgivings about catching the stray over food and confining it in a small carrier overnight until the shelter opened next day.

To our amazement, she offered to come over at whatever hour of the night the cat appeared and transport it directly to the shelter rather than wait until morning. She said nothing about payment or inconvenience; it was obvious that her first priority was for the welfare of the animal itself. Taking her at her word, we called at 11 PM the next evening, after we'd enticed the cat into a carrier. She arrived promptly, and, a half hour later, the stray was driven directly to the shelter where he would be protected, fed and cared for until - or if - someone reported him missing.

The next day, we visited the shelter to see how the new arrival was faring. All species of animals were being nurtured, some the victims of cruel abuse. One cat had been thrown from a moving car, and miraculously survived, though with a crippled leg. Another had been tortured with a match, someone's perverted idea of fun. Others had just been dropped off, their owners tired of them, thrown away like objects whose novelty had worn off. All were in the capable hands of a conscientious staff of employees and volunteers whose eye was neither on the clock nor on financial advantage but centered instead on the attentive concern that all these creatures desperately needed. As we visited, our emotions ran the gamut from heartbreak for some animals to hope for others. Above all, we were moved by the kindness all around us, a gentle force for good that had been directed toward the recovery of animals in distress and their placement with good families where they'd receive the love they had often been denied.

We returned to our home and entered into serious negotiations with our resident cat and longtime companion. Though it was paw and whisker all the way, our position was that the new cat - a stranger who'd appeared at our door several times in the dead of night, perhaps for a very good but yet unknowable reason - should come and live with us. Cato's position (or so it seemed to us) was a tentative and somewhat begrudging assent. At the very least, it would be an unexpected opportunity to show the best of human nature and introduce a little more compassion into a troubled world.

Someone once said that the true test of character is what we do when no one else is looking. In the current age, however, there seems to be a critical shortage of role models who demonstrate the kind of character that sets a positive example for others. To fill that void, many of us often look in the wrong places, focusing on political leaders, corporate CEO's, rock stars, and media idols, all of whom seem remarkably self-absorbed and concerned only with their personal aggrandizement. We were inspired instead by our experience with the shelter staff. We would provide a loving home not only for our own Cato, but also for the stray that had been visiting. He'd been rejected as of no worth; we'd right that wrong by taking him in, and the four of us would be happy together – at least that was our goal.

After visiting the tawny, short-haired cat several times at the shelter, and after more intense consultation with Cato, our Top Cat – during which, it seems now in retrospect we did most of the talking – we decided to adopt the new feline, whom we called Seneca, continuing our pattern of looking to ancient Rome for suitable names. We felt that there must have been a reason why he chose to visit us, night after night, and not any of our neighbors. We hadn't fed him, after all, and Cato was indifferent at best to his presence.

We thought at first that the odds were on our side. Both cats were neutered males, and each was somewhat familiar with the other, though there was an age gap: Cato was nearly twelve, and was only a kitten when we took him in. Seneca's history, of course, was unknown to us, though we guessed he was about three years old. We also know you just don't put one cat in with another, so we took certain precautions.

Seneca was introduced into the house when Cato was not present and then sequestered in a sanctuary room to get oriented and feel safe. It wasn't long, though, before our resident cat knew (or strongly suspected) that another cat had arrived on the scene, perhaps permanently. Several days later, his suspicions were confirmed when we thought it was appropriate for the cats to see each other since they had certainly smelled each other. It's not easy to read a cat's mind, and cats don't speak our language, but if Cato could have talked, he might have said something like "Aren't you happy with me? All these years we've been together, bonded companions, and now you bring in a stranger to share my space – and a much younger stranger to boot? What nerve – and what disloyalty!" It must be said that Cato had a valid complaint, and not only about the interloper whose energy and agility Cato used to have, and which he now saw demonstrated in a guileless and very overt manner.

Though few of us like to be confronted with our biological replacements, that simple truth can go unnoticed unless the example is close to home. When I described the situation to my niece, she said, "Well, Uncle Don, how would you like it if Page brought home a new, much younger husband?" Though it wasn't exactly the same situation, I immediately saw her point - and Cato's as well.

Cato soon became a very unhappy cat, and his displeasure manifested itself in physical form, or more precisely, in the language cats use. He began to exhibit behavior we'd never seen from him before - growling and hissing, elaborately marking his territory with copious eliminations, scratching numerous trees (the marks and the scents from its paw pads are a cat's "No Trespassing" signs), eating Seneca's food as well as his own, blocking the new cat's path whenever possible, and on more than one occasion attacking and driving Seneca away. There was no mistaking the fact – Cato's unwelcoming message became increasingly clear and unequivocal, and we were now beginning to dislike the actions of our own long time feline companion. We kept saying "There's enough space for both of you." Cato kept saying, "Who invited him?"

We had initiated and continued to follow an elaborate protocol to increase cat harmony. We fed them from different bowls and in different places, and if the cats were warily sharing the same location, Cato always got served first to show that he was still the Top Cat. We also petted him first, washed our hands, and then petted Seneca. We'd read that the order of affection was vital and had to be scrupulously observed because these graceful, elegant animals have a hierarchy that needed to be recognized and respected.

However, week after week passed, with no improvement in sight. Cato was feeling angry and displaced, and constantly on edge from patrolling his territory; Seneca was feeling unwanted and bullied despite the love we were developing and showing for him. We, of course, were in the middle. It was not a good place to be.

We asked for advice from the shelter staff. We were doing most of the right things, it seemed, but there had to be something more. A cat specialist in Portland was recommended, and that in turn led to a cat behaviorist who advised us to apply dabs of oil of lavender to cat spaces, give Cato doses of a combined flower extract that would reduce his aggression and increase his tolerance, and use a diffuser to disseminate friendly cat smells called pheromones. Some of this may sound far-fetched (the lavender smelled nice and at least made *us* feel calm) but we were determined to try every possibility to make things work and reduce the tremendous stress that everyone in the house – human and feline – was now feeling.

We read a very informative book about cats, and though we had done most things right, we learned that when we brought Seneca into our home, we should have had the two felines exchange scents through a neutral medium by rubbing a clean sock against the new cat in one room and leaving it in another room for the resident cat to inspect. We also read, in more than one place in the book, that no matter what humans did, some cats prefer to be solitary pets and will reject any newcomer no matter how determined or informed the attempt might be.

We began to realize that, alas, Cato must be one of these, and, upon reflection, why shouldn't he be? We'd raised him since he was a tiny kitten, he was the only cat we'd ever had, and he saw no reason for a change. What we thought was consent on his part was really disapproval, and until his wishes prevailed, there would be two very unhappy cats and two very unhappy people.

We had the best of motives: to rescue a creature in distress and offer him protection and security. But in the process of doing so, we had unintentionally threatened those very qualities upon which our oldest furry friend had depended. Day after day, week after week, the crisis deepened. Our home was permeated by a dramatic increase in tension, accompanied by a rapid decline in tranquility. The fault lay mostly with us because we had approached the whole situation backwards, making a decision first and then doing our homework on cat behavior afterwards. I was the culprit here, and I should have known that while after-the-fact research is better than none at all, it's not much better.

My heart had ruled my head, as it had with Cato, but this time with a very different outcome. Looking back, if we had simply put ourselves in Cato's place, we could have predicted that, just as we liked our privacy and wouldn't be happy with a permanent houseguest, - especially one we hadn't invited - then neither would he. It wasn't rocket science, but we'd behaved almost as if it was. Meanwhile, the feline wars continued, with no end in sight.

As much as we enjoyed Seneca – his leonine walk, his boundless energy, his playful nature, his supple, mid-air leaps, and his great affection – our strongest and clearest commitment had to be to Cato, who had grown up with us, indeed was growing old with us as well, and now preferred the peace and quiet of a nap by the woodstove to a romp in the meadow. Like many of us who've reached a certain age, he also didn't appreciate unwanted company, especially the kind that stayed too long or had the gall to actually move in. We had to face the fact that we had selfishly imposed our wishes on a fellow creature whose claim on us was far greater than any new arrival's could be, a claim that had to be honored, no matter how difficult that might be. We learned yet again that good intentions by themselves are simply not enough.

By the end of some seven weeks, the outcome was not at all what we expected. Whatever reasons Seneca had for choosing us, they were not what we had thought. We had to set aside what we wanted and do instead what was best for each cat. A very difficult choice had to be made, and we were the ones who would have to make it.

It was a very hard day when we returned Seneca to the shelter. His short span of years has been full of setbacks and rejection, experiences to which we had now unwittingly added, even though that was the very last thing we had in mind. I wrote an article about him that was published locally, and someone read it and adopted him.

It was comforting at least to know that he would have a new life and be safe and cared for, in the loving home that he had deserved for so long - but we would always regret that it could not be ours.

We would think about him often, recalling the joy his innocent, youthful exuberance gave us, wondering if now he was well and happy, hoping that he was loved and enjoyed as much by others as he had been by us.

And we would always miss him.

Cato

Co-founder and charter member of
The Stony Point Whisker Club

Noble cat, steadfast companion, faithful friend

Seneca

Dinnertime in Bristol Maine –
Cato patiently awaits another helping

*Out of harm's way - Cato on the beam
by his catwalk at home in Bristol*

Cato inspecting his grounds in Bristol

Regal Cato

*Master of all he surveys – a vigilant Cato
after a Maine snowfall*

The room at the Knox County (Maine) Humane Society which we helped fund in Cato's name. It was a way of dealing with his loss as well as providing for other animals in need.

Clio

10

A Philosophical Travel Cat

Cato, of course, would *not* miss him, and still remained on high alert. Having his territory invaded once meant that it could also be invaded again, possibly at any moment, thus creating a state of affairs that obviously required constant vigilance. For what seemed like a very long time, Cato sniffed his way around our house, checking every nook and corner, patrolling our property – that is, to say, *his* property – and warily approaching every crevice and hiding spot that might conceal a strange feline. Eventually, he decided that the danger was past, and that his human parents, disloyal though they had been, had learned their lesson, and could again be trusted.

Though Cato did not shed the weight he'd gained from eating Seneca's food as well as his own, he became friendlier, less wary, and, as he had often done in the past, shared our bed at night, often napping on his preferred choice, the lamb's wool afghan that Page's grandmother had crocheted for her. When he didn't sleep with us, we felt deprived. Seeing him at rest between us or at our feet and sensing his presence on our bed at night made us happy and content that we were a family again. All was forgiven, though perhaps not entirely forgotten.

Soon, Cato again enjoyed his home in Maine, and we enjoyed it with him. Inspecting his domain was part of his daily routine. In winter, he'd use the path I shoveled for him around the house and savor the great outdoors even in snowy conditions. During other seasons, Cato seldom left our wooded five acres and could often be found in the side yard, resting nearby under a clump of small evergreens. Cato, after all, was born outdoors and always felt very comfortable being there, regardless of the weather. Even during the heaviest rainfall, he'd be safe and dry outside under our porch, watching the birds and chipmunks, waiting patiently for the storm to pass so he could come back inside. Even though he was almost never very wet, we threw a bath towel completely over him, as we had first done when he was a kitten, and dried him off. I don't know which of us enjoyed it more – Cato for the loving attention, or us for his gentle purring that thanked us and approved of our actions.

As one year ran into another, Cato experienced what is all too familiar to humans of a certain age – he began to slow down and had some difficulty going up stairs. However, he also developed into a philosophical travel cat, enduring with the stoicism of any ancient Roman the car trip that we made to South Carolina on three occasions. My sister-in-law and her husband had bought a condominium at Seabrook Island, near Charleston, South Carolina and invited Page and their father to visit one winter; they both flew down, though Page could only manage to get away for a few days.

Seabrook Island was a beautifully landscaped little resort village with several miles of unspoiled beach – just the place to escape to during the rigors of a long winter or that time of the year in late March and early April known in other parts of the country as Spring but experienced here in Maine as a climatic no-man's land affectionately referred to as "Mud Season." Page thought I'd love Seabrook. As it turned out, she was right, but it wasn't that simple.

The problem was that I had great difficulty traveling. For years, our practice had been to hire a pet sitter for Cato whenever we went anywhere, but it was difficult and expensive to find someone responsible who would stay overnight. Even then, I was still anxious about Cato and would call daily to make sure he was all right. Page finally decided that the only way we could travel and enjoy ourselves was to take Cato with us. We could drive from Maine to Seabrook in two very long days, and Page felt that while Cato would not love car traveling – most cats don't - he would adjust so long as he knew that he was with us.

I held a different view. If I didn't like traveling, surely neither would Cato. After all, the only car trips he'd made in his cat carrier were moving to Maine with us, and going to see the local veterinarian - not exactly his favorite destination. It was suggested to us that if we rewarded Cato with a treat even after a short trip, he'd associate traveling in the carrier with something pleasant. That bit of elemental feline psychology proved to be very useful and made Cato less resistant. But the real problem wasn't with Cato – it was with me.

It was very stressful for me to leave home. I managed to come up with a seemingly endless list of reasons not to: our car could break down, someone might run us off the road, we wouldn't like it when we got there, Cato couldn't tolerate being confined for such a long period, *I* couldn't tolerate being confined for such a long period.

The list went on and on, each reason being less plausible than the last. Pushed to their logical conclusions, all my objections, real and imagined, ultimately meant we'd never go anywhere. The fact is, that living in Maine was a little like being inside the gate at Stony Point. No one seemed to be in charge of the world beyond it. There were more people, more traffic, more congestion, more tension, more of everything we'd moved to Maine to avoid; everyone was in a hurry, the pace was hectic, the noise startling, the conditions shabby and crowded. Maine had always looked good to us; it looked even better the farther away we traveled. Maine seemed unspoiled and pristine by comparison, and no matter where we went, we could hardly wait to get home. The fact is our adopted state spoiled us for other places. Maine wasn't perfection, but you could see it from there.

However, in the end, we did manage a twelve-day trip, four of which were spent on the road. As Page had foreseen, I loved Seabrook immediately. Cato did fine, settling down during overnight stays in unfamiliar motel rooms, an experience that might have been made easier because we used a special cat pheromone spray which neutralized the scents of any previous animals. At first, we were concerned how Cato might react to his temporary environment, but we needn't have worried. He would explore his new space, have a meal, and jump up on the bed with the detachment of one who accepted peacefully and without question or complaint whatever life might bring, and calmly look at us as if to say "I don't have a problem – do you?" It was clear that, as so long as we were with him, it didn't matter where we were - he trusted us and everything would always be all right.

We returned in successive years for a month at a time, and found a cottage to rent which was a little larger than my sister-in-law's condo and had a large screened porch that helped Cato accept not being able to go outside. He spent days and nights there, watching the birds and squirrels and chipmunks, as well as the occasional raccoon. The arrangement seemed to suit all concerned.

Fortunately, Cato was by this time a senior citizen pussycat and did not require a high level of activity. We were able to completely relax and enjoy his company on vacation, knowing that he was safe and sound. While he napped, we spent the days bicycling everywhere - in the village, to the local stores, and on the hard white sand of the beach, with occasional sorties into Charleston or the nearby area. Cato came through like the trooper he was, satisfied that if we were with him, whatever was happening was for the best, even if it was not his first choice of activities. Like any cat though, Cato saw no need for travel: his motto was "East, west, home is best," and was happiest when we finally arrived back home in Maine, put the carrier on the lawn and released him to his own stomping ground. He'd always make a close inspection of his personal turf, sniffing every bush and tree, just to confirm that he was home and glad to be there. I was tempted to do the same, and since we had no close neighbors, I probably could have.

Though some time had passed, the legacy of our abortive attempt to introduce a new cat into our home lingered on. While Seneca was in temporary residence, one of Cato's strategies to try to oust him was to eat his food. We had tried to prevent this but despite our efforts Cato managed to gain two pounds - a significant increase given that he weighed about thirteen pounds at the time. He had a largish frame, but was always a svelte kitty cat; now he was up to almost sixteen pounds and felt like a barrel. Many of us overeat when we're stressed, and Cato was no exception.

After we returned Seneca, Page and I worked on reducing Cato's weight by feeding him special low-calorie cat food. This appeared to have the desired result, but around the same time we began to notice Cato drinking more water than usual. This was noteworthy because we almost never saw him at the water bowl; now he seemed to be there almost every time we looked.

He also seemed to be getting fussier about his food, so we tried changing varieties and offering him delicacies to spark his appetite, but Page was becoming suspicious that he might have diabetes. Then one day, she ran her hand over Cato's back and felt his bones protruding through his skin. Not since he was a very young cat years earlier had he weighed so little. Our concern had now become fear.

11

Lengthening Shadows

We contacted our local veterinarian about Cato's condition and were told to get a urine sample, but Cato was not very co-operative. He was basically an outside cat and used his litter box only in winter when it was too cold to go out; now it was early fall, and he saw no reason not to utilize the great outdoors. After a few failed attempts, we finally got a sample and took it and Cato in for testing. The urine indicated an elevated sugar content, so a blood sample was taken which confirmed a tentative diagnosis of diabetes – Cato's blood sugar was over 400, much higher than normal. This explained the water consumption, the lack of appetite and the weight loss.

The vet recommended insulin injections, but everything was happening much too fast. Perhaps we were in denial that Cato was really so sick, and that somehow we'd failed to keep him healthy. Instead of medication, we wanted to try to manage the diabetes through a change in diet and were persuaded to purchase special food from the veterinarian for that purpose. Cato hated it. We asked our friends at the local organic pet store, and they recommended several other choices. Although he liked them a little better, he still was not eating enough and was becoming more and more listless.

We finally sought a second opinion from a different veterinarian, who repeated what we'd already been told:

Cato was indeed very ill and needed insulin. This vet was perhaps more persuasive, or maybe we were just ready to face reality. Certainly, he seemed more understanding about our concerns, and realized how important Cato was to us. We were taught how to raise a fold of skin between his shoulder blades and administer the daily injections with a small hypodermic needle. Although we were a little clumsy at first, Cato (as usual) tolerated this new indignity, and over time we all got used to the new routine. We gave Cato his first shot on December 16, 2006, and though we understood why we had to do it, we were reluctant and somewhat squeamish. We should have profited by Cato's example. At a level that humans may not understand but have often experienced in relation to their own health, he knew that what we were doing was for his own good.

Following the vet's advice, we started with a small amount of insulin twice a day, and kept a careful record of when the shots were administered, how Cato reacted, and how much he'd eaten. The plan was to coordinate the injection with his meal, so that Cato would derive maximum benefit from the medication; eventually, Cato would sit by his dish and position himself so we could give him the insulin more easily. Cato soon realized that his daily injections would always be followed by something good to eat - and, having made that connection, he'd often come to us at "shot time" with an expectant look.

As a result of Cato's illness and his need for medication, our lives changed radically. We were now tied to a schedule that required us to be home (and alert) at approximately 7 AM and 7 PM for his morning and evening injections. Our friends were tolerant when we explained we would be late for a dinner engagement or that after we arrived, one of us would have to go home, give Cato his shot, and then return. Our priorities about Cato had been established long ago; his welfare would always come first. If we cared for him when he was well, we would certainly care for him when he was sick.

Cato's diabetes also meant that when we traveled to South Carolina with him, we had to find motels en route that would not only accept a pet, but also provide a refrigerator in the room to store his insulin. The vet advised us to skip Cato's morning injection when we were on the road because the insulin would make him hungry, and if he ate, his stomach might be upset, and he could get sick in the car. Cato accepted this change in his routine with his usual philosophical resignation. After he got his evening shot, we gave him special treats to try to compensate for the confinement of car travel. Then, when Page had returned with some fast food, we all sat in the motel room eating dinner together, a ritual that made even a strange place seem a little like home.

Everything seemed to be going smoothly. Cato regained weight (a little too much, in fact), and his sugar count improved. We purchased a home glucose testing kit and, with a lot of trial and error, learned how to use it. The test had to be performed after Cato had fasted overnight and before his breakfast and the first injection of the day. This was really hard on all of us. Page and I are not exactly in top form or well coordinated in the early morning, and Cato was hungry and therefore not in the best frame of mind either.

The glucose test required three separate (though mercifully small) blood drawings – one at fasting level, another two hours later, and the third after three more hours; each sample was "read" from a sensitive test strip inserted in the glucose meter which calculated the blood sugar level. We'd select one of Cato's ears, making sure it was not the same one each time, and warm it with a wet cloth to improve the circulation and increase our chances of getting the blood sample we needed the first time around.

At first, it was an ordeal because of our inexperience, and we were tense and anxious. Later, we became a bit more proficient, but even under the best of circumstances, it was a lengthy procedure. Nonetheless, Cato endured these medical necessities with his usual stoicism. Sitting on his haunches, he would patiently and silently await our ministrations, not happy but assured that we had his best interests at heart – a conclusion he reached long ago and never doubted.

After six months or so, our dexterity had improved, our feline companion's glucose level was being carefully monitored, and much consultation had occurred with our veterinarian. We were still medical amateurs, but all three of us – Page and I and Cato – had accepted needles and injections as a fact of life. When we tested him in June, after our return from South Carolina, we had his blood sugar right where it should be, and Cato seemed to be his old self, although less active, but that was not surprising for a cat of his age. In July, on Page's birthday, Cato and I decided that perhaps The Whisker Club was a bit *too* exclusive. A motion was made - and passed unanimously - to reveal the secret paw shake to her, not only as a special token of our esteem, but also perhaps as a prelude to full membership - subject, of course, to her continued good behavior.

Then, some weeks later, Page and I began to notice Cato drinking far too often from the water bowl again. We both wanted him to be well, and tended to minimize what we were seeing, but it was clear that his thirst had resumed. We also found that despite several topical treatments and a couple of baths, we could not rid him of fleas. The unremitting onslaught of these parasites was relentless; they had sensed some weakness in Cato that was unknown to us but which they were all too willing to exploit. It was yet another disturbing sign that might have signaled dire consequences, but we were not prepared to accept the increasingly obvious fact that Cato's health was starting to deteriorate and that our best efforts were beginning to lose their effect.

What happened next is still a mystery. In mid-August, both Page and I had to be away from home most of the day. This was unusual, but there was no reason for us to worry about Cato being alone in the house. The weather was good, and he had plenty of food. Page left early; when I left a bit later, I made sure his cat door (which occasionally got stuck) was working so he could come and go on his own. Page got home first, in late afternoon, and found Cato upstairs in his bed under the eave behind her desk, a place he normally didn't use in summer. When I arrived home about two hours later, she had already checked on him and he seemed sleepy but otherwise fine.

After our dinner, Page saw Cato leave his bed and head down the stairs; it was apparent that something was very wrong. He was dragging his right hind leg behind him, the paw bent with the pad upward. Page hurried to pick him up and carry him downstairs. He didn't seem to be in pain and in fact wanted to go out, but that would have been difficult and probably not safe since he could barely walk, and if he had to, certainly couldn't run.

What could have happened while we were gone, and, of all times, on a day when we were both out of the house for an extended period? The only possibility that came to mind was that Cato had jumped and injured himself. But Cato no longer jumped, and had not for some time. For him, as for us, the shadows had begun to lengthen. He was now largely a sedentary pussycat, living in semi-retirement, still watching birds, squirrels and chipmunks, but no longer pursuing them. How and why could he have leaped and gotten hurt?

The following day we took him in for an examination; our usual vet was off, but Cato's leg was X-rayed. We were told there was no break, though there might be a sprain, but the actual nature of his injury wasn't clear. He was given medication, and we brought him home. Later Page found a faint trace of urine on his bed, something that Cato, being the fastidious cat he'd always been, would never have tolerated. We hoped that his injury would heal, but we still wondered how it could have occurred, and we were beginning to feel unsettled. A sprained leg was one thing, but the turned back paw, suggesting a lack of control, was another. Could his injury have been misdiagnosed? Was it, in fact, the result of a stroke and therefore an indication of a much more serious condition? Our doubts were beginning to grow, though we would never learn the truth.

We moved his litter box to the main floor and took to carrying him around. Inside the house, Cato spent most of his time in one of our closets, sitting in a dark corner, but when the weather was fine, he wanted to be outdoors, and we carried him out to lie in the grass, which he loved. He'd always preferred the lawn by the side yard, close to the path squirrels had worn on their way to the bird feeders on our deck, where they waged constant battle with their feathered competitors for food. From the sun porch, I'd keep an eye on Cato, moving him from sun to shade, and then bringing him in for the night. Meanwhile, his appetite began to be noticeably less.

A few days later we performed a scheduled glucose test. We were wary of the results, and our suspicions were confirmed: the numbers were back in the out-of-control range. The vet recommended a slight increase in his insulin and suggested that we repeat the test in two days. We followed his advice, but my anxiety level was approaching the out-of-control range as well, and my usual coordination had been replaced by a persistent clumsiness. Because the ear prickings were always somewhat awkward, several attempts were usually necessary to get enough blood for the test. Now even more were required. Cato's blood sugar continued to be unacceptably high, and he didn't want to eat. We tried tempting him with his favorite goodies; he nibbled, but food that he'd always liked had now lost its appeal.

In the early hours of Wednesday, August 22, 2007, around 4 A.M, long after we had gone to bed, I was awakened by a noise. At first, I thought an intruder was in the house and awakened Page. The sound was followed by a prolonged groan of agony. I raced downstairs, and found Cato near his litter box in the bathroom – he'd lost control of his bladder, and was having what appeared to be a seizure. I immediately thought he was in hypoglycemic shock, a condition we'd been warned might occur if his blood sugar was too low. Cato's latest glucose test had shown just the opposite, but we had no time to ponder this discrepancy - Cato was in pain and we needed to help him as quickly as we could. I grabbed a bottle of corn syrup - pure liquid sugar that we'd kept for such an emergency – and dabbed some inside Cato's mouth. That appeared to help; at least his agony seemed to be less. We called the veterinarian's after hours phone number, and even though it was now nearly 4:30 A.M., spoke to a very helpful doctor who, based on what we told her about Cato's medical history, concluded that his attack was related to diabetes and that we'd done the right thing.

Still, it made no sense. His blood sugar had just recently been tested, and it was high, not low: if it had suddenly plummeted, we wanted to know why. We felt the helplessness that many others have experienced as they've watched someone they love in pain, not knowing what's happening or what to do. We saw how Cato had suffered – and we knew we never wanted him to suffer like that again.

12

Taking Him Home

The danger clearly was far from over. Something was very wrong, and we needed to know what it was so we could help our beloved companion. We moved him into an adjacent room, and we slept downstairs with him, occasionally stroking him to assure him and ourselves that somehow everything would be all right. What little rest we had the reminder of the night was fitful, and next morning we called the veterinarian's office and arranged to bring Cato in as soon as they opened. We put him in his carrier, and drove off, with Page sitting next to him in the back seat so she could pet and comfort him. She noticed that Cato was grooming himself and settling down, content as always that we would continue to do our best for him as we had in the past; content, too, that when his need was greatest, we could be trusted to do everything in our power to make him well.

Later that day the veterinarian called us to report that Cato was very sick. He had severe anemia, almost no oxygen in his blood, and had probably developed pancreatitis, a condition that often resulted from diabetes and which was difficult to treat in cats, particularly elderly cats. Moreover, he'd had a second attack. He'd be given a blood transfusion, further tests would be conducted, and they'd let us know next day if he was any better. The vet also cautioned us that we might have to make a very difficult choice. His warning was the implied answer to the questions I'd framed countless times but never had the courage to ask: was diabetes invariably fatal? No matter what we did, would it, in the end, claim this special feline who meant so much to us and who had graced our lives for so long?

The vet informed us he had a commitment that would take him out of town the next morning, but he would check on Cato and call us before he left. Another doctor would be there during the day. I remember asking if anyone would be at the clinic overnight if Cato took a turn for the worse and needed immediate treatment. I was told that no one was on duty after hours: I could only hope that nothing went wrong, because if it did, there'd be no one there to deal with it. The thought made me even more anxious and concerned. Cato had been away from us overnight only once before, many years earlier when he was a kitten and had gotten sick. Now, the house seemed very empty without him; though we knew it was for the best, he'd been entrusted to the care of strangers – medically trained strangers, but strangers nonetheless, for whom he would be just another patient, one among many. He would not be with us, his human family, we who had raised him as if he were a child, and who already missed his quiet friendship, his steadfast devotion, his reassuring presence.

True to his word, our vet called at 7 A.M. the next day to tell us that Cato had come through the night but had not improved. His survival thus far was encouraging – a slim piece of good news that we clung to - and now we wanted to see him and comfort him. Page called the clinic to ask if we could visit Cato in the afternoon.

91

We were both in fairly good spirits and tried hard to be optimistic, but as we were ushered to the part of the clinic where we expected to find Cato, I noticed that the assistant who was leading us there seemed ill at ease. We saw the cage where he'd been confined, but his body was under a towel, with only his tail showing. Previously, there had been some discussion about providing him with a heated blanket, so perhaps that was what we observed. Nonetheless, I asked why he was covered.

The assistant was shocked. "Cato died this morning," she said, "didn't you know?" and gestured toward the chart on the wall, the same one which also indicated that we had planned to visit. "Cato died at 9 A.M. " it stated. There must a mistake, we said. Then we saw the notation on the smaller chart, near where he lay. "Died in cage," it said. It was August 23, 2007.

No one had called us.

We were devastated. A black hole opened suddenly beneath us, and we plunged into a dark chasm of heart-wrenching despair. It had no bottom. Instead of being able to see Cato and console him while he was sick, we were shown instead his body covered by a towel. In that awful moment, our hope turned to desolation, and we were beside ourselves with grief; we both openly wept, the wave of our emotions a mix of sorrow and anger - sorrow that our beloved cat was gone, anger that we had not been told. The wall chart should have indicated that we'd been contacted; the absence of that information should have been a clue that we had not. We hadn't been there with him during his last moments, and human error had left us unprepared for his death.

"Died in cage" – that final, cruel impersonal phrase, that terrible clinical statement, bereft of feeling, indifferent to pain and loss and rage- seared itself into my consciousness - how I had wanted to say goodbye, to tell Cato again how much he meant to us, and that if he had to die, to have him die at his home, unconfined, surrounded only by those who loved him.

At some point, the attending veterinarian came over, and told us that Cato had suffered a third attack that morning after our regular vet had called us, and this last attack had been fatal. She apologized because we hadn't been told and asked what we would like to do with Cato's body. I had no doubt. "We're taking him home," I said, and that's what we did; gently, lovingly, through our anguish and heartbreak, we carried our old friend back to a place he knew, a place where he belonged, a place that was his as much as ours.

13

Hail and Farewell

We buried Cato in our side yard, in a place where he loved to nap, along with some of his toys and wrapped in a favorite towel we'd always used to dry him off. Working through our tears, we did the most difficult thing we've ever had to do. As we placed him in his grave, we petted and brushed him one last time. For his marker, we used a large boulder shaped like a headstone that we'd unearthed from his burial spot; it lay deep in the ground, seemingly waiting to be discovered and serve its purpose. We also planted a forsythia bush nearby, like the one he always enjoyed at Stony Point and which provided him with the shade and shelter he often preferred.

The poet Robert Frost once observed that all he knew about life is that it goes on – and so it must. But anyone who's ever felt about an animal the way we did about Cato knows it isn't easy. We tried to deal with his loss by establishing what we thought of as mileposts – things to do that would keep us on the road to recovery. We donated his toys, his remaining food, and the medical supplies we used for his diabetes to the animal shelter not far away in Thomaston. We started an album for his pictures, and for the notes and cards that people sent us. We also contributed toward the establishment of a room at the shelter in his memory.

Sympathetic friends and neighbors have described Cato as a member of our family, and so he was, but that term is far from adequate. There ought to be more accurate words than "family" or "pet" in our language to describe the relationship between animals and people which, in many ways, is better than that between humans. Interactions with animals are generally simpler and more direct. Human to human is more complicated, often more time consuming, and perhaps less satisfactory for all the effort that's involved.

There are very few individuals, for instance, from whom we can expect unconditional love, and members of our own species can disappoint us – and we them – in ways we've all experienced. By contrast, the bond with an animal can be very different, as we learned with Cato. The trust and comradeship, as well as the simple affection and uncomplicated love, can be superior to all others, making their loss all the more difficult to bear.

Cato lives on in photos and reminiscences, and I believe that his spirit lives on in some way as well. Albert Einstein concluded that energy is never lost, and I believe that too. Richard Bach has also written "A farewell is necessary before you can meet again. And meeting again, after moments or lifetimes, is certain for those who are friends."

We think of our devoted feline often, recalling those days at Stony Point nearly fifteen years ago, where we found each other and he shared his life with ours; the late summer afternoons at the battlefield where the three of us enjoyed each other's company amid the sweeping views of river and bay; the countless times his playful antics made us smile and be thankful for the pleasure he always brought us; the quiet evenings huddled together by our woodstove during the Maine winters, warmed in more ways than one against the cold of the night.

Some day, in some place and in some form, we will meet our cat again. In a way that perhaps cannot be explained or even understood, somehow we will know him, and he will know us.

Until that time, *Ave Atque Vale, Felis Nobilis* - hail and farewell, noble cat, loving companion, good and faithful friend.

Renaissance

Lives have a great deal of similarity, so much so that it's virtually impossible to find one that is totally unique. For that reason, perhaps readers may have experienced for themselves some of the common threads that have run though this narrative, ones with which we are all so familiar that they might be considered universal: making mistakes, for instance, that we have to live with because we can't undo them; accepting the unpleasant but realistic fact that our judgment can be grievously wrong; striving to control an outcome when that control is not only irrelevant but obstructive; setting standards for ourselves and others and failing to meet them because they are unrealistically high; and realizing that good intentions by themselves are not enough - in other words, the whole litany of human shortcomings as they relate to the difficult, often painful, ordeal of personal growth.

Someone once said that if you asked an animal what time it was, the reply would be "now." Our answer would be more complicated, and probably less accurate. The human concept of time is certainly very different. We think of it as sequential, though we've all had the experience that some events which happened long ago are as real as ever and seem much more recent than they actually are. All of what's been written so far, for instance, is as true as memory can make it, and even though some of took place nearly fifteen years ago, it is as vivid as if it had just occurred. That's not surprising. The power of recollection is common to us all, so much so that it belies our society's convention of minutes and hours, the numbered days and years of the calendar, the inexorable sweep of the clock's hands. We fret about the past, we worry about the future, and we try to deal with the present – and, though they are constantly in flux from one to the other, we generally think of these constructs as separate and distinct with discrete identities in spatial terms – the *past* behind, the *present* in front, the *future* also in front but far off.

A similar view of time might be understood as specific locations on a linear chart: the *past* faintly visible on the distant left and moving away; the *present* clear and in front, constantly filling from the future, yet forever flowing into the past like a kind of time trough; and the *future* always approaching, vague and indiscernible on the distant right.

Yet it may not be that way at all. In Kurt Vonnegut's *Slaughterhouse Five*, the main character, Billy Pilgrim, an American prisoner of war in Dresden, Germany in 1945, as was Vonnegut himself, is transported to the imaginary planet of Tralfamadore and learns about their concept of time:

"All moments, past, present and future, always have existed, always will exist. The Tralfamadorians can look at all the different moments just the way we can look at a stretch of the Rocky Mountains, for instance. They can see how permanent the moments are, and they can look at any moment that interests them. It's just an illusion we have here on Earth that one moment follows another one, like beads on a string, and that once a moment is gone, it is gone forever."

In that sense, Cato will live as long as we do, and as long as those who read these words, and we can see him in his best moments whenever we choose, and still enjoy the pleasure of his company. And when we had difficulty accepting Cato's death, wondering if we'd done all we could for him or whether we'd been remiss in some way, I found solace in another passage from *Slaughterhouse Five*:

> *"Earthlings are the great explainers, explaining why this event is structured as it is, telling how other events may be achieved or avoided . . .All time is all time. It does not change. It does not lend itself to warnings or explanations.*
> *It simply is."*

Poetry also offered some comfort. Not for the first time, I read Robert Frost's *West-Running Brook*, a colloquy in which a husband speaks to his wife about the contrary ways of nature:

> *". . .Some say existence like a Pirouot*
> *And Pirouette, forever in one place,*
> *Stands still and dances, but it runs away;*
> *It seriously, sadly, runs away*
> *To fill the abyss's void with emptiness.*
> *It flows beside us in this water brook,*
> *But it flows over us. It flows between us*
> *To separate us for a panic moment.*
> *It flows between us, over us, and with us.*
> *And it is time, strength, tone, light, life and love –*
> *And even substance lapsing unsubstantial;*

> *The universal cataract of death*
> *That spends to nothingness – and unresisted,*
> *Save by some strange resistance in itself,*
> *Not just a swerving, but a throwing back,*
> *As if regret were in it and were sacred.*
> *It has this throwing backward on itself*
> *So that the fall of most of it is always*
> *Raising a little, sending up a little.*
> *Our life runs down in sending up the clock.*
> *The brook runs down in sending up our life.*
> *The sun runs down in sending up the brook.*
> *And there is something sending up the sun..."*

I didn't know what this life we live was all about, but I believed it had to be about something. The whole gamut of human experience - the joy, the despair, the disappointments, the loss, the pain and the hope – must have some meaning, some relevance to a reality outside ourselves. Frost's lines reminded me that there was indeed "something sending up the sun" - some logic, plan or pattern that wasn't always easy to discern and somehow far too easy to doubt.

Living with Cato, caring for him, and missing him made me realize that each life makes a difference, for good or bad. Either the world is a little better or a little worse for our having lived; we either give or we withhold - no act or omission is neutral. Above all, through his presence and my inability to forget how he came to us, Cato reminded me that whatever pretensions I had to always being a good person and making the right moral decisions, there was a serious defect that had to be corrected first - an ethical blind spot that had clouded my vision. I was not an evil person, and I certainly wasn't perfect and never would be, but I wanted to be better than I was; like all of us, I had made good choices as well as bad ones, but my priorities were centered on myself, and that focus allowed me to overreact on that day in 1993, taking the life of a creature who had done me no harm. I had the power to hurt, and I had deliberately chosen to use it.

It wasn't very complicated, and it certainly wasn't a new concept, but somehow I'd overlooked it and failed to acquire a crucial attribute – the ability to understand the feelings of someone else, be it human or animal, and imagine myself in their place. As the writer Alexander McCall Smith has stated, such understanding was "the beginning of all morality.... Inflicting pain in such circumstances would be like hurting oneself."

Smith also writes about understanding "at the most intuitive, profound level, what it was to be a human being, which is not easy. Everybody could do evil, so easily; could be weak, so easily; could be selfish, so easily." He concludes that "the giving of love, this sharing of the heart, is what redeems us, what makes our pain and sorrow bearable."

Those words provided some consolation, but still we missed our cat terribly. It was very hard to live again in his home, not to look for him in his favorite places, knowing instead that he now lay near the forsythia whose shade he would never enjoy. And we missed The Whisker Club, now permanently dissolved. The black hole of despair was always just a hair's breath away; we balanced precariously on its edge, trying hard not look in and be engulfed by its flood of paralyzing hopelessness. We rarely succeeded. In our grief, no matter what we did, we always returned to the undeniable fact that we were so much the less for Cato's absence.

I thought about the ancient pattern of mortality - death as a balance to life, the bloom of nature countered by its inevitable fading, beginnings completed by endings, the eternal predictability of the seasons - and I wondered whether all the joy Cato gave us over the years was worth the pain we were experiencing now. Despite all we had done or could do, the seemingly endless void, the empty place in the heart, was still there, and felt like it always would be.

Then we talked to Judy Garbow.

Judy is an animal communicator whom we had contacted, telling her about Cato and sending her a picture. On Tuesday, November 6, 2007, she came to our house at our request because, despite doing almost all we could do to move past the loss of Cato, we still grieved for him and wondered if somehow we could reaffirm our bond with him. None of this is as implausible as it may appear. Could there be all the vital presence of life and then suddenly none at all? Where there had been light and sound, could there now be only darkness and silence? The connection some people can feel for each other and which we had with Cato can be so strong as to seem impossible to be severed completely. I had never had met an animal communicator before, but I also knew that skepticism can be a hindrance to a belief that might well be valid. In our continuing attempt to recover from the loss of Cato, Page and I wanted to consider all the possibilities to address our grief, even ones that to others might seem strange or even bizarre. It was more an act of completion rather than desperation. We simply wanted to make sure we had done all that we could do.

After seeing some more photos of our cat and being in his environment, Judy told us that she was able to sense positive vibrations from our feline who had known that it was time to leave – was that the reason, sick as he was, that Cato was so calm during that last ride to the veterinary clinic? – and that he still loved us. He also wanted us to get another cat, one that we would love and care for as we did him. Cato told Judy that the new cat would be female, that we wouldn't have to look for her – she would find us – that we'd know her when we saw her, and that we should be receptive for her arrival, which would be soon. The cerebral, rational/logical side of my brain thought, at least briefly, that all of this was exactly what anyone in our situation would want to hear. Another, larger part of me - that part that needed healing - felt comforted and open to the possibilities suggested by our cat through Judy. We would simply withhold judgment; we would be receptive, as Cato wanted; we would simply wait and see.

We didn't have to wait long. Three days later, on the evening of November 9, I got an e-mail from Tracy Salas, director of the Knox County Humane Society in Thomaston. She knew about Cato and how we felt about him; she also knew that we didn't think we were ready for another cat because we had told her so several times. Accordingly, Tracy had never contacted me about adopting a new cat, and she and Judy were unknown to each other. Yet now, Tracy was telling us that a stray female had come to the shelter and perhaps we'd like to see her. The attached photos took our breath away –

the stray looked just like Cato. We were told her name, but the images were what remained fixed in our minds. Page and I glanced at each other – could this be happening as Judy said it would – and could it be happening so soon?

The next day we drove to the shelter. The stray's disposition was uncannily similar to Cato's - friendly, affectionate, yet regal and elegant without being aloof. Again, we were told what her name was, and this time it had the impact it should have had the first time.

This shy, lovable orange tabby, probably a year old or less, this sweet-natured animal who'd been rescued from a life on the streets, had been given a most unusual and yet appropriate name, the meaning of which was beyond debate or denial or willful misunderstanding. That name was Renaissance. That name was Rebirth.

Was she Cato returned? I asked her that question as I petted her in her cage at the shelter – she turned her head, and, for the first time, her eyes looked directly into mine. I had my answer.

Epilogue

We brought Renaissance home a few days later. She is now part of our family, though she has undergone a name-change. We've called her Clio, for the muse of history in Greek mythology. History, after all, is nothing if not continuous, and she is now part of Cato's story and ours too.

We believe Cato's spirit lives on in her. The day we brought her home, she scampered from room to room, raced up the stairs to the catwalk and our bedroom as if she'd been there before, had left for a short while, but had now returned. Most cats would have found a safe, dark place to hide until they felt comfortable. She felt that way almost immediately.

Clio is as active and playful as Cato was when he was younger, and is naturally possessed of a wonderfully intense sense of curiosity. Though she resembles him in many ways besides appearance – demonstrating on several occasions, for instance, that she can also sense danger well in advance of its approach - she has her own personality and has restored laughter and joy to our household. How she came into our lives continues to be a source of amazement to us, one that isn't readily explained by chance or circumstance.

Why, for instance, was Renaissance given such an unusual name - one that suggested a completion of the events that had occurred up to that point, removing any of our doubts about adopting her? Why had the shelter director never contacted us before about adopting a cat, and then suddenly did so only three days after Cato –

through Judy – had told us to be watchful for a new feline? Remember, too, that Judy and the director were strangers, and had never met or communicated. Cato had been right about everything, including his belief that we were ready for another cat, something we had firmly denied on several occasions. Not for the first time, he knew better than we knew ourselves.

How this whole unpredictable journey came about – from the years at Stony Point battlefield and the arrival of Cato, our life with him in Maine, Cato's last illness, and finally what could be called his renaissance in a creature that embodies some of his spirit and much of his character - might be for some a matter of conjecture, but Page and I would have to ignore the depth and intensity of our own experience not to feel that there are forces, levels of energy, and perhaps entire dimensions at work in our lives and in the world that we had not been aware of and did not fully understand.

In some quarters, this may be labeled as superstition. It could be argued, however, that our culture's way of life - its technical expertise, and its emphasis on material goods and temporal success - may blind us to other ways of seeing. Science is only part of the truth, and perhaps only a small part at that. There are also many other things that make the world what it is, and we often fail to notice them, although they are always present, patiently awaiting our recognition and acknowledgment.

We were glad when Clio arrived, but we still mourn Cato and will never forget him. He was our steadfast companion – the kitten romping by the forsythia, the feline of regal bearing gracing our presence, the staid, older cat spending his last years with us, the kindred soul intertwined with our own.

Now, there remains only one thing left to do. Cato told Judy that he wanted me to write a book about our journey together. That book has now been written.

Nothing is ever really lost, or can be lost.
No birth, identity, form,
No object of the world, Nor life, nor force,
Nor any visible thing;
Appearance must not foil,
Nor shifted sphere confuse thy brain.
Ample are time and space —ample
the fields of Nature.

Walt Whitman, <u>Leaves of Grass</u>

A former teacher of English, Don Loprieno has maintained a life-long interest in education and history. For nearly twenty years, he developed and implemented interpretive programs for two Revolutionary War state historic sites in New York's lower Hudson Valley: New Windsor Cantonment and Stony Point Battlefield, where he was also site manager. In 1996, he received an Historic Preservation Merit award for his role in the restoration and relighting of the Stony Point lighthouse, the oldest on the Hudson River.

Since January 2001, Don has lived in Bristol, Maine with his wife Page and their cats Clio and Titus, where he is active in community affairs, writes a column for the local newspaper, and has become a strong advocate for animal rights. In 2004, based on new research and primary source materials, he wrote *The Enterprise in Contemplation*, the first comprehensive account of the battle of Stony Point in over a hundred years.

The Stony Point Whisker Club is his second book.